Heal through

A year around the medicine wheel

Learn to connect with your ancestry

T0103201

A
52-WEEK
GUIDE

INDIGENOUS WISDOM

VALERIE RINGLAND PhD

ROCKPOOL

With gratitude and respect for the Walbunja and
Brinja-Yuin peoples, spiritual sovereigns of the land where
this book was written, and Gulaga Mother Mountain
for her unconditional love and support.

A Rockpool book
PO Box 252
Summer Hill
NSW 2130
Australia

rockpoolpublishing.com
Follow us! **f** 🄾 rockpoolpublishing
Tag your images with #rockpoolpublishing

ISBN: 9781922786203

Published in 2024 by Rockpool Publishing
Copyright text © Dr Valerie Cloud Clearer Schwan Ringland 2024

Copyright images © STC 2024
Copyright design © Rockpool Publishing 2024

Design and typesetting by Sara Lindberg, Rockpool Publishing
Editing and index by Lisa Macken

All rights reserved. No part of this publication may be reproduced,
stored in a retrieval system, or transmitted in any form or by any means,
electronic, mechanical, photocopying, recording or otherwise, without the
prior written permission of the publisher.

A catalogue record for this
book is available from the
National Library of Australia

Printed and bound in China
10 9 8 7 6 5 4 3 2 1

Contents

Opening

Thank you for opening this book. I invite you to take a journey with me to deepen your understanding of yourself.

If you do not identify as Indigenous, this book is for you. Although Indigenous peoples around the world struggle to survive in Western culture, we have generously shared traditional cultural knowledge with outsiders. This book will help you understand these struggles more deeply by supporting you to connect with your own Indigenous ancestry and have a better general understanding of Indigenous cultures.

If you do identify as Indigenous, this book is also for you. There are resources on Indigenous social science that prompt you to think about how to apply traditional teachings to modern life so you feel more whole in Western spaces. There are also exercises and teachings shared from other Indigenous cultures that can help you see your own culture more clearly, including commonalities across Indigenous cultures as well as beautiful diversities of individual cultures. This book may also help you see more clearly some ways you and your culture are still colonised and provide you with insight and tools to heal some of those wounds.

This book is designed to be your companion over the course of a year, wherever in the world you may live. After a year of working through this book you will be able to more fully embody the spiritual meaning of the word 'sovereignty' and feel a deeper peace about yourself and your life. There are stories to inspire you and help you feel seen, and exercises to facilitate you to do things like connect with your Indigenous ancestors as well as ancestors of the lands where you live, divine your medicine wheel, integrate sacred earth-based rituals and ceremonies into your life and experience more grounding in your body and the land where you live so you feel more solid and centred.

There are many spiritual books that offer tools to manifest whatever you want. This is not one of those. Much of what we desire has been corrupted by collective and individual traumas in our subconscious. We cannot be ourselves until we unpack the energetic suitcases we are carrying with tools that allow us to process and release their contents. To survive today, we must learn to walk in two worlds: the world of our holistic Indigenous cosmologies, and the modern capitalist Western world.

If you would like to sync your reading of this book with seasonal moments (solstices, equinoxes and cross-quarter moments), please refer to the appendix at the end of the book. Though the book is written with a year-long journey in mind, you may prefer to read straight through or open at random and read when you are moved to. There is no right way to use this book. Only you may determine the right way to live your life. It is spiritual abuse for anyone to tell you otherwise. May you be enriched, enwisened and blessed throughout this journey and beyond.

WEEK

1

Indigenous science

WEEK BEGINNING: _____

SEASON: _____

The word 'Indigenous' refers to both a cultural group whose beliefs, traditions and ways of living originated with connection to a specific place, and to people with a holistic worldview who see life as cyclical and have a conscious awareness of an inherent interconnectedness of being.[1] We will work with both understandings in this book. We are all humans and have Indigenous roots somewhere on Earth, but our ties to our country and culture may be lost or fractured. It is important to be aware of our differing realities and journeys.

Science is the study of knowledge. Most of us think of science as men in white lab coats with test tubes. If that includes you, here is an opportunity to decolonise your mind.

EXERCISE

Speak, draw or write your associations with science, then read on.

Western science is rooted in an ancient Mesopotamian and Egyptian decision to split natural and supernatural causes of events. This was taken up further by ancient Greeks and Romans, then revived by Islamic scholars in the mediaeval era. The scientific method and experiments as we know them began around the 1500s in Europe, and the Industrial Revolution of the 1800s brought into being many institutions and professions of Western science. (If you'd like to learn more about this history, Wikipedia's article on 'science' has a good summary.)

The root of the Latin word 'science' is 'to know', which comes from an older root word meaning 'to cut or split'. This is why a Western scientist trying to gain knowledge about a butterfly will describe the environment of its capture, then kill and preserve a specimen to do things such as measure its dimensions, look at parts of it under a microscope, document the patterns on its wings and label it with a Latin title. It is a way to know through cutting or splitting the butterfly from its environment.

Indigenous science has never engaged in this split. It offers a holistic perspective for building and testing our knowledge. Instead of cutting or splitting the butterfly from its environment to gain knowledge, we build a relationship with the butterfly within its environment. Using all our senses and allowing our understanding of our self to be changed, we become intimate with the butterfly and the environment.

Indigenous science is our birthright, our deepest ancestral inheritance. The following principles of Indigenous science come from Oneida-Gaul scholar Dr Apela Colorado:

- ⊙ nothing is objective
- ⊙ non-humans are included in our study
- ⊙ study is done as a ceremony
- ⊙ time is nonlinear and cyclical
- ⊙ relationships are privileged
- ⊙ it is holistic, drawing on all senses: spiritual, emotional, physical and mental
- ⊙ it is healing and ends with feelings of peace, balance, vitality
- ⊙ at the end of a journey we feel more fully present and embodied
- ⊙ humour and light-heartedness are an important part of the process.[2]

EXERCISE

I invite you to reflect on your holistic senses (spiritual, emotional, physical and mental) in an exercise my husband Lukas Ringland created. It helps us get a visual baseline of where we are in this moment. Using the diagram below, intuitively place a mark farther from the centre in each quadrant indicating how strong or at peace you feel in that aspect of your life. Then connect the marks.

PHYSICAL   MENTAL

EMOTIONAL   SPIRITUAL

This is a reflection of your (im)balances at the start of our journey together. I suggest you take a photo of this or keep it in the book so you can reference it again later on.

In nomadic cultures when people moved around a place throughout the year, it made sense to mark seasons by celestial moments. Around the world and across cultures, Indigenous science practices have honoured solstices, equinoxes and other celestial events. And as people developed deeper relationships with a place, it became important to create ceremonies and stories honouring a nuanced understanding of seasons based on local weather patterns, animal movements, the planting and emergence of food sources, and spiritual rituals. This included marking times of year to avoid certain foods too, like no fishing during breeding season out of respect.

Western science may sometimes be practised with awe, less often with humility and rarely with reciprocity with our non-human friends. Indigenous science does not allow us to play God by placing ourselves above other beings. There are no existential hierarchies. On the contrary, as one of the youngest species on the planet, we are expected to learn from older, wiser beings who have survived here a lot longer.

WEEK

2

The medicine wheel

WEEK BEGINNING: _____

SEASON: _____

Indigenous cultures around the world are based on a philosophy of innate wholeness of all beings. The medicine wheel is a cross-cultural 'essential metaphor for all that is'.[1] Walking the medicine wheel describes our life journey. Representations of the medicine wheel in physical form are used as a tool for learning, growth and remaining in balance.

A common representation of the medicine wheel is a circle divided into fourths[2] (though some cultures such as in China and India divide the circle into five, and others such as the Celtics divide the wheel of the year into eight). For now we will start with the most common wheel with four directions and some of her metaphors: directions (north, east, south and west); seasons (winter, spring, summer and autumn); times of day (morning, afternoon, evening and night); stages of life (infant, child, adult and elder); elements (earth, air, water and fire); and aspects of being human (physical, spiritual, emotional and mental).

All directions need to be in balance for us to live well and be centred in our hearts. To visualise the medicine wheel in three dimensions, imagine a central point below the ground, a point in the centre of the circle representing the heart that unites us all, and a central point above the ground. The portion of the medicine wheel above the ground represents Father Sky, the visible parts of life, and the lower half of the medicine wheel represents Mother Earth, the invisible parts of life. Mother Earth is experienced through feeling and intuition; she is mysterious, a dark womb of life. The famous image of the Vitruvian man[3] based on a classical Greek medicine wheel may help you visualise your body as a medicine wheel.

EXERCISE

Wherever you are now, orient yourself to the directions north, east, south and west (perhaps with the help of a compass app on your phone). Take a moment to face each direction and acknowledge it, then take a moment to acknowledge the Earth below by touching the floor, the Sky above by reaching up and the centre by bringing your hands to your heart.

You have now done a simple practice of an embodied medicine wheel. I have done an extended version of this practice for many years to start my day and have worked with others who do a basic version such as bowing in the four directions to start theirs. It is a lovely way to integrate the medicine wheel into your life and honour your body as an altar, as well as to increase grounding and centredness.

Inside the medicine wheel are known aspects of a culture and individual's world. What is outside the medicine wheel is without form, the Unknown. Energy is constantly cycling around the medicine wheel. For example, we may walk outside to stand in the sun (physical) and feel gratitude for the warmth on our body (emotional). We may have an experience of deep peace (spiritual) and notice a thought bubble up that says 'It's a beautiful day' (mental). In this simple moment our energy has moved around each direction of the medicine wheel and into the centre of the circle, the heart. It is in the heart that we reconcile energies we receive from the Earth below and Sky above. You may have heard about two-legged humans walking on the Earth's surface being called channels, hollow bones or human lightning rods because our way of moving through the world connects the energies of Earth and Sky.

EXERCISE

Building on week 1's exercise, you will now gain more insight into where and why you may be in or out of balance. Using the wheel below, take a few minutes to free write and intuitively create a reflection for yourself of your mental, physical, spiritual and physical worlds in this moment. Reflect on the nature of what is going on in your mind, your spiritual world (that is, what is giving your life meaning and purpose), the emotions you are experiencing, what is going on with your body and in your environment. Include a few words about what centres you and helps keep your heart open.

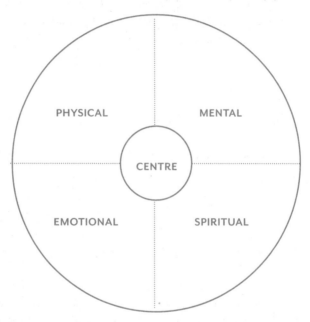

Looking at your four-directional medicine wheel reflection, consider what area(s) might need attention and care. This is a tool I developed that can be used periodically as a check-in. Consider how you are spending time keeping your heart open and yourself centred. You may wish to bookmark this page and come back to this exercise again in a few weeks or months to chart your progress towards balance.

WEEK

3

Core values

WEEK BEGINNING: _____

SEASON: _____

Our values impact the way we live our lives. They are rooted in our culture(s), lived experiences and beliefs, and they determine our daily priorities. Look at the medicine wheel you filled in for week 2. What is at the centre? If you wrote nouns like 'family' or verbs like 'playing soccer', what underlies them? Perhaps 'family' is based on valuing safety or trust and 'playing soccer' may be based on valuing passion or teamwork.

EXERCISE

Make note of your core values. Reflect on how you
embody them, how you live them in your daily life
(mentally, spiritually, emotionally and physically).

When we are living our core values, it is easier for us to be centred. When we are centred, we feel more relaxed and are able to access flow states where our lives seem to be filled with synchronicities. In Indigenous science, synchronicity is the way time is measured. You can't force an egg to hatch, or will the winter to be over. These things happen or they don't, and no amount of force will change that. There's power in these natural processes, and we can embody that in our daily lives and be just as authentic as our non-human relatives.

Being authentic is being centred in our hearts. And it is easiest to freely be ourselves when we feel safe (physically, mentally, spiritually and emotionally). Of course, there will always be some unsafe feelings in our lives, but for most of us it is hard to be authentic when we are feeling unsafe for extended lengths of time. Adrenaline puts us into survival mode, commonly involving behaviours of fight, flight, freeze and fawn. Some of us have normalised feeling unsafe and suffer from adrenal fatigue[1] or sleep troubles, or struggle to trust ourselves and others and question the foundations of our faith. Human life is messy, and acceptance of this is vital to creating safe space for yourself and others to be vulnerable. To build safety into your life, maintain some space for messiness across all aspects of the medicine wheel.

EXERCISE

Ask yourself when, where and with whom do I feel safe emotionally? Mentally? Physically? Spiritually? Notice what insights arise. If you regularly feel unsafe with yourself, in your home or with people in your inner circle this is important to be aware of.

Reflect on how well you allow yourself and others to be messy emotionally, physically, mentally and spiritually. Where is your empathy, compassion and humility about the human struggle strong? Where are your limitations and common triggers? Where are your hard boundaries?

Keep in mind that allowing messiness means accepting reality, including your and others' limitations. It does not mean making excuses for abuse or neglect. Our hard boundaries also reflect our core values.

Sometimes we are taught our core values, and sometimes we gain them through lived experiences. Someone may have grown up being able to trust the word of their family and close friends, but then had a partner who cheated on them. How deeply that person values trust may be reflected in the amount of pain they feel when that value is brought into conflict with their partner's behaviour. They may feel so betrayed they do not want that person in their life anymore, or they may so deeply value fidelity they work to rebuild trust or change the boundaries of their relationship.

Being authentic is also easier when we feel grounded. We're going to imagine the medicine wheel in three dimensions now. Using the Vitruvian man from week 2, look at the centre (or core) of the body in the wheel. It looks to be at the belly button. (There's a reason doing abdominal crunches is said to strengthen our core!) Imagine the Vitruvian man body mapped onto a tree of life image: from the belly downward, the human body is underground.[2] (If you know about chakras, or energy centres in Hinduism, you will find this familiar, with the heart at the centre of the upper and lower chakras.)

Aspects of life that are invisible, intuited and mysterious are often referred to as the 'sacred feminine'. We get data, or information, about these aspects through the four clairs (clairsentience, clairaudience, clairvoyance and clair cognizance).[3] Aspects of life that are visible and represent the upper part of our bodies, including our arms and head, are often referred to as the 'sacred masculine'. They are related to the five senses (seeing, hearing, tasting, smelling and touching). The visible aspects of life are often emphasised more in the modern world, while invisible aspects of life such as values, myths and stories and beliefs are taken for granted or assumed.

However, for a tree grounded in earth, how well it grows depends on the quality of its soil, its relationships within its environment and its access to basic sources of nourishment like sunlight. We humans are similar. Just think of a time in your life when you were in an environment that allowed you to thrive, and compare that with a time when you struggled much more. A potted tree can only grow so big, and similarly when we feel constrained we either get stuck and make sacrifices to survive or we move to change our environment with gratitude for having legs!

Like a tree, if we overdevelop the visible aspects of life we will feel shaky, get caught in the breeze of a momentary whim and may even lose some branches or parts of our lives if we are not careful. If we overdevelop the invisible aspects of life, we may starve our bodies of important nourishment and struggle with basic survival needs. The medicine wheel teaches that it is wisest to focus more than half our energy on creating a strong grounding and ensuring we are living our core values. The idea is that then what emerges in our lives will come from this strong invisible foundation into the visible world,[4] which will help us maintain balance and teach us how to err when we are in doubt.

EXERCISE

When, where and with whom do you feel strong in yourself (emotionally, physically, spiritually and mentally)? When, where and with whom do you feel more in your body and less in your head?

WEEK

4

Grounding or earthing

WEEK BEGINNING: _____

SEASON: _____

We noted in week 3 that to embody the medicine wheel we need to focus more than half our energy and attention on the invisible aspects of life. This allows us to stand with strong legs, hips open and relaxed, connected with the Earth. We commonly talk about carbon footprints, but what about our physical footprints?

EXERCISE

Prepare to do a short walking meditation barefoot or in flat shoes. Walk in a small circle as gently and softly as you can. Look up a fox walking video if you want an example of gentle stepping. You may wish to imagine that your feet are caressing Mother Earth with gratitude with each step. Notice how this feels and compare these movements with how you normally walk through the world.

For many thousands of years, we humans have been walking barefoot or with leather-soled shoes and sleeping on a mat on the ground that keep us energetically connected with the Earth. It is only recently that so many of us have been spending time in high-rise buildings, wearing rubber-soled shoes and sleeping on elevated and energetically ungrounded mattresses. All of these changes have literally disconnected us from the Earth and elevated our anxiety levels through an increase of ungrounded heady energy.

A number of Western scientific studies[1] suggest that grounding or earthing ourselves reduces pain and anxiety and helps regulate cortisol cycles.[2] Cortisone is called the stress hormone because it helps our bodies respond to crises, wakes us up in the mornings and regulates our metabolism, among other functions. From an Indigenous scientific perspective, the importance of spending time with the Earth is obvious. When we are physically present with loved ones, able to hug them and share a meal together, for example, it feels very different from when we are connecting through a voice or video chat. When we walk by a tree in a park on our way to work, or sit on the grass for a picnic on the weekend, this feels very different to living intimately within a forest, building a shelter from fallen limbs and leaves, being able to predict changes in weather, witnessing patterns of seasonal change, hunting and gathering our food and leaving offerings at sacred sites.

I am not intending to romanticise our ancestors' lifestyle but to point out that, for most of us, our intimacy with the Earth has diminished. While electricity and gas in our homes have certainly made our physical lives more comfortable, they have also disconnected us from our natural environments and thus from parts of ourselves.

For Indigenous peoples the land under our feet is the source of our traditional culture. I have heard some Indigenous people describe our feet as our eyes into Mother Earth. If we are spending our time in rubber-soled shoes in buildings insulated from the Earth, disconnected from our sacred Mother, then our culture is literally ungrounded and it is not surprising we spend more time in our heads than feeling deep peace in our bodies.

There are many ways to practise grounding or earthing ourselves. I encourage you to do at least one of the following for a few minutes every day and observe how you feel:

- ⊙ Stand or walk barefoot outside.
- ⊙ Sit, lie or sleep on the ground outside.
- ⊙ Wear only leather-soled shoes.
- ⊙ Use a grounding mat on your bed or at your desk.

You can both make and buy grounding or earthing products such as shoes and bed sheets. Traditional moccasin shoes are leather soled, as are many traditional sandals in Europe and Africa, and traditional shoes in parts of Europe and Asia are wooden soled.

Other ways to ground ourselves may be less literal but are equally as important. Doing physical activities that feel good in your body such as dancing, gardening, walking in the wilderness, swimming, patting a pet or even having sex can help us embody our core values and be grounded in ourselves more fully.

EXERCISE

Take a look back at your medicine wheel exercise and core values from weeks 2 and 3. Is there an activity that helps you feel vital and strong in yourself that you could spend more time doing? Is there something you could let go of to facilitate this way of honouring yourself?

In addition to feel-good physical activities, we can work creatively within our modern environments. If we sit by a screen much of the day or live far from the sea there are creative ways to bring that healing energy into our lives. Salt lamps use a small amount of electricity to emit similar energy as if you were standing by the sea. Soaking our feet or bathing in saltwater at home can help us ground and relax into our bodies. If we live in the inner city and hear traffic more than birds or the sea, we can play ocean waves or forest sounds inside our homes while making our breakfast in the morning. There are many freely available videos online that can lull us to sleep or help us be more grounded during a hectic workday.

Finally, we can honour the power of our imagination. I like to start my morning routine by visualising roots extending from my feet into the earth below. Sometimes when I'm stressed, I close my eyes and imagine a safe or sacred place in the wilderness where I have felt deep peace. Simply imagining ourselves in such a space can calm us down and ground us more in our bodies. The following exercise is a quick way to bring ourselves back into our bodies if we are spiralling out.

EXERCISE

Pick a place you remember well enough to visualise yourself being there. Imagine yourself there: how it feels, what you hear and smell and what you see in your surroundings. Close your eyes and connect with this place for a minute or more. When you reopen your eyes, notice how you feel and the state of your mind. Take note of a few safe and sacred places to visit in your mind when you are stressed.

WEEK

5

Ritual and ceremony

WEEK BEGINNING: _____

SEASON: _____

There is a power that each of us can embody that cannot be cultivated through the intellect, through reading and writing (though I realise the irony of writing this in a book). This power is based on our connection with the Earth and our faith in an unseen, interconnected sacredness in the world. When I refer to power, I do not necessarily refer to forcefulness. When we look at the Earth, sometimes there are forceful powers expressed, like earthquakes, volcanic eruptions or monsoons. But more often I experience more subtle powers – such as the beauty of a flower opening her petals, a bird fluttering leaves as it moves to another branch in a tree or the continuous babble of a brook flowing over rocks down a hill.

I see ceremony as intentional embodiment of the sacred through physical action in spiritual community. Another explanation is 'Processes that are place-based, in relationship with the natural world, which draw together past, present, and future into a space in which personal and collective transformations occur. The focus is on balance and harmony among a vast network of relationships.'[1]

Since Indigenous science is experienced directly through our relationships with ourselves, each other and the invisible world, we do ceremony to gain knowledge, purify ourselves and honour ourselves and others. During ceremony we use our physical bodies and the natural elements of fire, water and air, and of the land such as minerals and wood. Ceremonies create opportunities for deeper healing, connection and being in the world. We may do ceremony in communion with other humans or not, but we always do ceremony in community. Even when we are physically alone, we are never existentially alone, as we are surrounded by non-human beings, elements of nature and our ancestors. Ceremony reconnects us with ourselves and the Earth, strengthening and affirming the links between our spiritual and physical worlds. As Tiwa Elder Beautiful Painted Arrow Joseph Rael says, '[If] we find life empty or unsatisfying, [that's] because we don't do enough ceremony.'[2]

Ritual and ceremony are similar but different. A ritual is a consistent action done with intention. We create rituals around that which we hold sacred (in high esteem or value most) in our lives. Rituals create peace and stability and tend to be more mundane. For example, I value my physical health and do rituals such as washing, stretching, hiking and brushing my teeth to take care of my body. I value my spiritual health and do rituals such as meditations, prayers, offerings and smudging my home to take care of my spirit. I value my intellectual health and do rituals such as reading, reflecting on different perspectives, and creatively playing with ideas to take care of my mind. I value my emotional health and do rituals such as listening to music, sharing my feelings with loved ones and expressing myself through art and music to take care of my emotional world.

We often create rituals without realising it. For example, many people have rituals around coffee and alcohol. Understanding why we are doing such rituals, what is driving us, is empowering. If someone realises that what she is holding sacred is taking a break from the office more than a caffeinated drink, she may take a walk or do a short meditation at her desk instead of going to get a coffee. This may allow her to feel more fulfilment in her break and bring more sacredness into her ritual.

EXERCISE

Reflect on a ritual you perform every day, something you consider mundane. What values and intentions are you expressing through that ritual? What need or desire are you meeting?

Reflect on your safe and sacred space from week 4. What helped you feel sacredness there? Is there a way to create some of those feelings with a daily or weekly ritual?

Ceremonies may be made up of rituals, but they are based in metaphorical understandings of the way the world works. Ceremonial rituals grow in power through social acceptance and repetition over time. For instance, there are some Zoroastrian temples in Asia where fires have been continuously burning for over 1000 years. To Zoroastrians, fire symbolises purity and the brightness of God, and they express how much they value that by keeping alive a flame that was lit after a year of purification practices done by their ancestors. Unpacking all of the intentional metaphors of meanings underlying a Catholic christening or a traditional Hindu wedding ceremony may be a bit more complicated, but the idea remains that there are shared metaphorical meanings imbuing those ceremonies with power.

Let's unpack a ritual within a ceremony you are likely familiar with: a woman being married wearing a white wedding dress. The white dress was popularised by Queen Victoria in 1840 when she married Prince Albert. White was not the style of the day, with people in Europe preferring more colourful dresses that could be more easily reworn and laundered. Wearing white became a status symbol to show you could afford to have a dress made for your wedding ceremony that you would only wear once. White also symbolised purity and innocence, values that were upheld in the Victorian era. While a white wedding dress may mean something different to you, by being aware of the metaphors underlying this tradition, we are empowered to choose whether continuing them feels right today. (I chose to wear a red silk wedding dress, which to me symbolised a start to my marriage with passion and a fiery spirit.)

EXERCISE

Reflect on a ceremony you are familiar with such as a wedding, baptism, birthday or graduation. Choose a ritual and consider its underlying meaning, including historical perspectives about the ritual's inception and modern changes. How well do that ritual's metaphorical meanings align with your core values?

Indigenous science is based on sustaining our ceremonial connections with the land and elements of nature, with an underlying metaphorical understanding that all life is sacred. Acts such as killing an animal are traditionally imbued with giving thanks to the animal's spirit and promising to use its meat, bones, skin and fur to the fullest to honour the life it was giving up.

EXERCISE

Consider your connection between ceremony and the Earth,
how you express gratitude to the earth, air, fire and water and
to the trees, plants and animals that sustain your life. How do
you honour the sacredness of your human nature?

WEEK

6

Honouring our ancestors

WEEK BEGINNING: _____

SEASON: _____

An Indigenous Elder in the Amazon told me that the vast majority (he estimated 90 per cent) of the thought loops that circulate in our minds are not based in our ego, but in ancestral trauma. This has rung true for me and many people I have worked with.

Blood and/or adoptive lineages are the most common way we think about ancestry, reflected in a family tree. But ancestry is so much more. I think about ancestry in four ways:

⊙ our blood and/or adoptive lineages
⊙ the lands where we work and live
⊙ the lands, cultures and religions we sustain a strong spiritual connection with
⊙ personal karma (past, present and future versions of our selves/identities).[1]

Ancestry of place includes where we were born and have lived and live now, and may include places where the people in our family lived if they were there for a long time. When you think about your ancestry I encourage you to reflect on this definition, keeping in mind also that in animism and evolutionary theory in Western science, ancestors are not limited to humans!

If we go back far enough in our ancestry, all of us are Indigenous to somewhere. On my father's side my Indigenous ancestry is Frisian from northern Germany (East Frisian), and on my mother's it is Sumerian from southern Iraq (Ashkenazi Jewish). Indigeneity on my father's side was clear to me from an early age; growing up, I was taught some cultural traditions and lore and spent time visiting the marshy, swampy and often cloud-covered country near the North Sea.

My mother's indigeneity was hidden beneath layers of trauma and Jewish religion, as well as generations of living in Eastern Europe and the US. It took me many years to make peace with Judaism and see more clearly the Mesopotamian roots of biblical stories. I then started seeing scary mythological figures in my dreams, which led me on a journey of learning what I could about ancient Mesopotamia and the Indigenous cultures that live(d) there. I found that I feel at home among the lore and country of the Sumerians too (which is also swampy, but much hotter than Friesland).

With Indigenous German and Jewish blood, and being born and growing up on land in the US where slavery and Indigenous massacres took place in the recent past, I have experience healing a lot of ancestral trauma. When the Amazonian Elder told me that 90 per cent of the thought loops in my mind were due to my carrying ancestral trauma, I wanted to let it go and bring more peace into my world. But how?

We wouldn't be here if not for our ancestors, and every culture has ways of honouring ancestors. Every culture may not, however, consider ancestry as fully as in the definition above, and we all have some unhealthy and traumatised ancestors that need healing, as well as some ancestors with dignity and integrity. The first step I suggest to honour your ancestors is to create a container for them, a sacred space in or around the home. I have found that when we do not maintain an altar outside of us, our bodies become the altar by default, and seeing ourselves through all the projections of our inheritance can be very challenging.

A powerful practice to connect with our ancestors is to create an ancestral altar. An altar is a space for doing ritual and ceremony, where we set up symbolic objects that bring strength and meaning into our lives, leave offerings and draw strength by maintaining sacred space. As my ancestry is full of trauma, I wanted to create space to show I was in relationship with my ancestry, rather than allow the trauma to be carried in my body and seeping into my everyday life. When I began an ancestral altar practice years ago, I created one human and one non-human (tree) altar outside my home. Over the first few months two of my human ancestral altars were completely destroyed during thunderstorms. I was so grateful that the trauma and violence had left my body! And I noticed that I no longer was attracting car accidents or tripping or bumping into things as much as I had in the past.

My ancestors settled down after regular offerings and ceremony, and today I have the ancestral altar inside. Some ancestors I honour directly; for example, today I burned a candle to honour the birthday of my best friend, who passed away six years ago. Some ancestors I honour through rituals for healing; for example, earlier in the week I made two yarn dolls to represent people in my family who are lost in abuse and denial, and when it feels like the right time, I will burn the dolls with the intention that such energy be transformed and reborn into a healthier form. I also have an altar for my baby girl when as a parent I'm not clear what to do for her.

EXERCISE

Choose a space in or around your home. Consider whether a container or drawer you can close or an open space such as a shelf feels better. Reflecting on the full definition of ancestors above, intuitively add items that celebrate your ancestry. Add items for healing, things that remind you of deceased family and friends, objects that remind you of a specific time or place and photographs or written names to commemorate important people, places and events.

Reflect on your cultural heritage and items that express your core values. Set boundaries, such as intending to connect with supportive or healthy ancestors.

Leave an initial offering of an object of beauty such as a crystal, flower or candle, or something special such as a piece of chocolate or a bit of wine. Your ancestors are receiving these offerings energetically, so I suggest disposing of food and drink afterwards as they will have lost vitality through your intentionality.

Whether you use an ancestral altar or not, your ancestors receive the intentions of your offerings. Honouring someone through dedicating a work of art or doing a good deed, or honouring ancestors of a land by planting trees, are all beautiful practices. There is a saying among many Native American cultures that everything we do affects ancestors in seven generations in either direction of us. If that sounds impressive, many of those cultures define a generation by seven people (from your great-grandparent to your great-grandchild with you in the middle is one generation).

Connection and imagination

WEEK BEGINNING: _____

SEASON: _____

You may have created an ancestral altar after reading week 6, so let's delve deeper into what an altar is. *Altar* is from a Latin word for 'on high' (think altitude) and refers to honouring and worshipping through making an offering or sacrifice such as by burning leaves or incense and sending smoke upwards. The offering is a symbolic (in other words, metaphorical) expression of the biblical phrase 'let go and let god.' It is a way of expressing internal desires or prayers externally and sending them out into the world. Each offering requires a willingness to do our part to bring our wishes into being.

For example, while wishing to become a mother, I need to be willing to let go of some aspects of my current life (such as sleeping through the night and having a lot of alone time) to make space for a child. A few months ago, I sat down to play with clay and found myself making a mother holding a baby. I painted it and placed it on my personal altar to prepare me for becoming a mother and getting into alignment with my desire. At the right time I will remove the clay figure from the altar and ceremonially dispose of it using vision, intuition and insight. That is the process.

You may be wondering what the difference between an altar and a shrine is. Shrines are sacred containers (for example, the ark of the covenant) that honour the spirit of people, events and ideologies, from veterans of war to Hindu gods. Shrines are more contemplative spaces, while altars are more interactive spaces of worship. Most churches and temples are blended spaces, where people leave offerings like incense, flowers or candles on altars dedicated to figures like Jesus, Krishna or Buddha, and also sit in contemplation and pray for insight and guidance. I find it helpful to be intentional about these differences in my life, but blended spaces may work for you. Ultimately, what we do is build relationships with figures, ideas, events, places and energies, and those relationships flow when we both give and receive and do not always ask or give with an expectation.

Items intentionally placed onto altars are often called power objects, meaning they are imbued with energy and meaning. I put them on and take them off an altar with care and ceremony. Power objects can be anything that we feel drawn to or have meaning for us, from a candle to a cross to a rock we pick up off the ground. Sometimes the meaning is clear to me when I place an object on an altar, and other times the meaning becomes clear over time. Occasionally I am moved to break open power objects to free trapped energy, creating ease for my body and relationships that do not need to break since I am doing so metaphorically. I may also be moved to pass power objects on to other people, bury them or burn them. It depends what feels right and what insight comes to me in visions and intuition.

Indigenous science altars were traditionally built outdoors. You may have heard of the Incan rock mesa on a small island in the middle of Lake Titicaca, or of living tree altars in Europe made famous by Druids. Doing ritual and ceremony in wilderness, or even in a garden or park, is a different experience to being indoors. You can more easily get feedback from birds, insects and other beings, and from the weather. For example, I often speak with people who are working through challenging emotions while I am outside. Often the wind will rustle through the leaves of a tree or a bird will fly by at a moment that feels auspicious and brings insight or feelings of affirmation. A prelude to building an outdoor altar, though, is a connection and relationship with the place and the beings who live there. Trees are generally receptive to relationships with humans, acknowledged in Western science through our symbiotic carbon-oxygen exchange of air.

EXERCISE

In the spirit of trees as living altars, choose a tree that is easy for you to spend time with. Set an intention to connect with that tree. Start by acknowledging the tree with a look, nod, smile or other gesture. Notice what you feel. Then touch the trunk, either with your hand or by leaning against it. Close your eyes and take a few deep breaths. Notice what you feel. Sit for a few minutes and experience.

Reflect on what offering you could give to the tree as thanks for sharing its energy with you. You may be moved to leave something physical such as a flower, or to sing for a moment while you're with the tree.

When doing something like this, how do we know when it is working or if we are imagining things? Let's consider how power objects work. Do you have a relationship with an object such as a childhood teddy bear or a favourite mug? How do you feel when you hold that object? While objects do have their own inherent energy, the warm feelings you have are primarily based on you projecting power into that object and creating a one-sided relationship. That's one way to connect, but if we create that kind of relationship with a person, it won't last very long. We need to show up with some openness and interest to learn about the other, and to share some of ourselves. Do you get a feeling or sense of knowing when a plant is thirsty or when your dog wants to come inside? When a relationship is working, there is reciprocity.

When we start opening up to relationships with our ancestors, the energy that emerges can overwhelm us. It's as if we had stuffed part of ourselves into a closet, and upon opening the door a bunch of energy was set loose to flow more freely in our lives. This is only empowering if we maintain a sense of agency about it. I have found that it helps many people to manage this energy by designating an ancestral spokesperson. Usually it is someone familiar to the person, such as a recently deceased relative. Opposite is a protocol for designating a spokesperson, and you can find a guided meditation version online.[1]

EXERCISE

Bring an offering to your ancestral altar. Then sit at the altar and introduce yourself energetically. Let your ancestors know that you will be starting to work intentionally with them and that you require a spokesperson who is able to offer you support, protection and patience. Let them know that is the one you will communicate with and that all messages need to go through the spokesperson.

Ask your ancestral spokesperson to step forward and introduce themselves so you can feel their energy. Ask them to show you a sign so you can tell when they're giving you messages or are in your presence. Make note of what comes to you, or what happens outside of you. If you are not clear now, ask for a sign again later.

WEEK

8

Reciprocity

WEEK BEGINNING: _____

SEASON: _____

Reciprocity is a basic tenet of Indigenous science and animistic living. It's based on exchange, but not the transactional kind like paying a few dollars to buy a burger. Reciprocity is grounded in generosity. One way to think about it is as follows: the Earth gives to us so that we may live. We get air to breathe, water to drink, food to eat and beings that can be sacrificed for us to eat, build shelter from and make clothing and so on. And what does the Earth get from us in return? In return, we take care of our environment, our human and non-human relations and the elements. You may be thinking, wait, but we don't do reciprocity very well – what about rainforest destruction and air pollution, deep-sea mining and other painful modern realities of human progress? We are already experiencing the effects in our internal and external worlds, because we are interconnected with the Earth.

The more connected we feel to another person the stronger the relationship, and the more hurt we feel when they are in pain. It's similar with pets or trees we befriend, landforms or places. I had a friend who was so intimate with her garden of 20 years she could feel specific plants calling to her when they were thirsty. If you do not identify as an Indigenous person or do not live on your people's land, try to imagine what it might feel like when people have relationships with plants, rocks, landforms, sacred sites, and their human ancestors over many generations for thousands of years. When Indigenous scientists say that we feel the pain of the land in our bodies, this is why.

You know that feeling when you walk into a room and realise something uncomfortable has happened there? Lands carry those feelings too, and places need healing just as much as we do. The Myall massacre site in Australia is a place where people have gathered regularly for years to pay respect to those who died and take responsibility for their ancestors' roles. Recently a monument was built there, and some of the Indigenous Gamilaraay people say that the land feels safe to visit again.[1]

This works at an individual level as well. There are reasons we are living in certain places, as we grow through interactions with our environments. As a child of a Jew and a German, it is not surprising that combination of trauma resulted in me experiencing profound abuse at home. Growing up in Atlanta, Georgia, with its recent history of Cherokee genocide,

African American slavery and Civil Rights leadership, provided me with a good external mirror for my painful and messy internal reality. The trauma inside me was reflected in the pain of the land and people around me.

EXERCISE

Reflect on a place you have lived for a while. What connections and disconnections do you feel with that land? What do you feel when you leave and spend time elsewhere, and when you return? What does that place mean to you?

In his book about restorative justice, Canadian crown attorney Rupert Ross reported with surprise that Ojibway people in Canada he worked with were confused by comparisons.[2] They told him that they don't walk through a forest and compare the cedar tree to a grackle bird, because both are unique aspects of creation, and they don't see competition or survival of the fittest, but mutualism, symbiosis and interdependence. Similarly, they don't compare people's gifts. Being a chief is no more valuable to the community than being a hunter or a mother. Everyone's gifts are valuable and worthy of being expressed. There is no existential judgement.

When we're not intimate with a place, it can be harder to see the interconnections there and to value the different species that keep an ecosystem healthy. Western environmentalists see 'nature' as a place to protect, keep pristine and separate from human intervention except for taking walks or camping. But Indigenous scientists see nature as a web of life we are all part of, and our role as humans in a healthy ecosystem is to be stewards and caretakers of the lands, waters, air and other beings. It's not that we should leave the land alone, but as one book title puts it we ought to be 'treading lightly'.[3] Aboriginal Australians do 'cultural burning' to clear brush so that animals like kangaroos can move through the land more easily (and more easily be seen for hunting), to support the procreation of eucalypts and other plants that rely on fire and to keep up the soil quality for root vegetables they cultivate.

This interconnectedness is built into Indigenous science and indigenous cultures. At the start of the book we said that Indigenous science excludes objectivity. This means people avoid existential judgement because to judge someone or something's worth is to put ourselves existentially outside the web of life. We are not individuals within a community, but a community made up of individuals. Indigenous science helps us experience belonging with each other, the land and other beings around us. Discord within one individual is seen as everyone's issue because it infects all relationships that involve that person. Consider the image and exercise on the next page.

EXERCISE

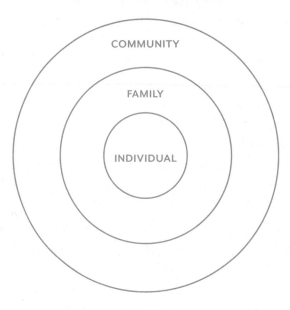

Reflect from the inside out and the outside in
about a topic of your choosing; for example:

⊙ Inside out: a child experiences trauma, creating secondary
trauma for family that didn't protect them and tertiary
trauma for community members who feel less safe.

⊙ Outside in: when a child experiences trauma it is seen as a
breakdown of healthy community boundaries. Community
members get together to discuss what happened and how they
can take responsibility to prevent future abuse. They discuss
who needs to step up and take more responsibility to ensure the
collective value of child safety is upheld, what support the family
and individuals in trauma need to heal and who can help them.

*What happens if you draw another circle around these that stands for
the land? Reflect on how that impacts us humans and our societies.*

....

....

....

....

WEEK

9

Wetiko

WEEK BEGINNING: _____

SEASON: _____

In week 8 we looked at sacred reciprocity, a foundation of Indigenous science. But what happens when someone is greedy and takes more than their share? Potawatomi scientist Dr Robin Wall Kimmerer explains: 'In the old times, individuals who endangered the community by taking too much for themselves were first counselled, then ostracized, and if the greed continued, they were eventually banished . . . [and] it is a terrible punishment to be banished from the web of reciprocity.'[1]

For Apalech scientist Dr Tyson Yunkaporta this teaching comes from the emu, the 'troublemaker who brings into being the most destructive idea in existence: I am greater than you, you are less than me . . . the source of all human misery.'[2] Aboriginal peoples across Australia organised their societies to keep this in check, using the emu's changing positions in dark constellations of the Milky Way as a way of connecting the lesson with the season. (A dark constellation is a constellation made up of dark space where there are fewer stars within the bright Milky Way.[3])

Many forces that have shaped the modern world can be traced back to this destructive idea taking form: that some people are *objectively* worth more than other people. Among the Anishinaabe, a monstrous energy called *Windingo* is an eternally hungry, destructive force that consumes without stopping, can never be sated and even eats its own kind.[4] The *Zar* spiritual disease in northern Africa is similar,[5] and among Indigenous cultures in Asia a disease is caused by poison in the mind that makes us forget who we are, showing up as anger, longing and ignorance.[6] What resonates most with me is what the Ojibway call *Wetiko*, a psycho-spiritual disease that separates an individual human ego from an interconnected self who knows its innate connection with all of creation. Wetiko is 'a cannibalistic spirit who embodies greed and excess'[7] and a psycho-spiritual virus, because that core destructive thought (I am greater than you, you are lesser than me) becomes enmeshed with a person's spirituality, meaning the person believes in it.

I have found that most of us carry a lot of Wetiko. We feel not good enough, alone and spiritually orphaned, and suffer from bullying and victimisation in a hyper-competitive world. We are living with the ongoing impacts of colonialism. Indigenous scientists describe colonialism as 'a violation of the psychological womb, a great rupture with the Mother [Earth], and a spiritual depression and moral suicide resulting in a systematic repetition of historical and generational failure'.[8] Thus, colonisers are traumatised peoples who became disconnected from an intimate, reciprocal relationship with their Indigenous roots and began re-enacting that trauma around the world. I do not remember where I read this Ojibway story, but I find it powerful: people say we died of smallpox and other diseases. But our Elders tell of the first French trappers our people encountered, how they had so much Wetiko that our whole community couldn't contain it, much less heal.

Sometimes we think as humans we are very different from other species, but consider trees crammed close together for commercial gain of the same species and age lacking connection with a network of elder trees and a sustainable ecosystem. Such trees do not communicate well with each other, compete to grow as fast as they can towards the sun, and suffer more disease than those planted in a forest with elder trees limiting their pace of growth by creating a canopy, and an interconnected root network to help each other heal from disease and share resources like water.[9]

We spend time crammed into desks in classrooms and offices with people our age, competing for resources, struggling to feel deeply interconnected with people and place. When we are part of extended kinship networks, spend time with Elders who hold space for us to learn and give us wise advice, who uphold the value of reciprocity such as teaching us to fish and only take what we need and remove all rubbish, we feel more connected to each other and to the Earth. Doesn't that sound similar to trees in a forest?

We can heal our Wetiko. It is tough work, because it requires us to redefine our egoic self-identity to re-align with our interconnected sense of self. I learned as an abused child that the world was not safe, that I have to protect myself and be intimate with dangerous people to survive. Healing Wetiko beliefs requires us to experience an alternate reality. As an adult, I set fierce boundaries for myself and build relationships based on trust, and I have had to disengage from members of my family, leave jobs without another lined up and endure financial crisis, end close friendships and do other things that were painful to uphold my values. This work takes endurance and grit, and teaches us our worth. Let's start today by unpacking one key aspect of Wetiko: human supremacy.

EXERCISE

Use Steffen Lehmann's image titled 'Eco versus 'Ego'[10] to reflect on human supremacy, on where you place yourself, family, community, country and humanity above the rest of nature. When do you feel 'Why me?', and when do you feel 'Why not me?' Notice when you feel victimised and where you lash out, when you feel shamefully lesser than and righteously greater than and where you see something as objectively true with no room for another point of view to exist. Reflect on what you can do to flatten the hierarchy of human supremacy.

Cosmology

WEEK BEGINNING: _____

SEASON: _____

In week 9 we began unpacking some beliefs about human supremacy, disconnecting us from the rest of nature and our non-human kin. 'Cosmology' refers to an underlying worldview that is based on a creation myth/story that illuminates core values. Because creation stories are foundational, they offer deep insight into how we perceive and organise our worlds. We each carry a collection of such myths/stories that inform our core values and beliefs to help us navigate our world and understand our place in it.

There's a saying that a knot cannot untie itself. Another way of thinking about it is, a fish cannot see its own water. When we are immersed in an environment and know nothing else, it's really difficult to see its limits and blind spots. Think about a time you travelled in the physical or through movies or imagination to a land and culture that was very different to yours, and how much you learned about yourself through experiencing so many new reflections. Much of cosmology is like this, very unconscious and subconscious until we are made aware of it.

Do an online image search for 'god'. Now search 'big bang theory science' (so you bypass the TV show) and, finally, 'Indigenous creation'.

I bet the image of 'god' was familiar: typical Judeo-Christian (and Eurocentric) Father Sky iconography of an old white guy in the sky. And for 'big bang theory science' you see some starbursts along with representations of Darwin's theory of evolution, a linear view of time that goes from 'primitive' bacteria to humans, the apex species. 'Indigenous creation' images seem more symbolic and less literal; many don't include humans at all, some look cosmic and may remind us of the Milky Way or a starburst and most are quite colourful.

I picked these three searches because they represent the strongest cosmologies in Western countries (Judeo-Christian and Western science), with Indigenous creation as a contrasting worldview that is the basis of Indigenous science. You may be asking yourself why Western countries have two. This is the modern manifestation of the split in ancient Mesopotamian between the 'natural' and 'supernatural' worlds, which we talked about in week 1. This dualistic/binary cosmology is composed of a 'supernatural' (Judeo-Christian) and 'natural' (Western science) aspect. When you think about all the binary views we have (good and evil, right and wrong) and how our legal system is run (guilty or innocent) you can see that dualism in action. Let's consider a few more common cosmological terms.

EXERCISE

What comes to mind when you see the phrase 'holy land' or 'sacred land'? What about 'holy site' or 'sacred site'? What about 'holy mother', 'divine mother' or 'sacred mother'? Does your mental image change with those different phrases? Do online image searches if you like and see how your mental images align.

Indigenous science is holistic, not dualistic. There is no objectively 'holy land', because all land is sacred. Babies are born and ancestors have died on all lands, but the lands where we have lived for generations are deeply sacred to us and our tribe, nation and people, who are intimate with that place. Through the land our metaphorical and literal worlds align: the natural and the supernatural are intertwined and whole. Taking care of our holy Mother includes reciprocity with human mother figures, as well as with the land and all of creation living there.

Some Indigenous scientists see the land as an ancient ancestor, a relative. Others see the land as their identity. Many cultural creation stories begin with a divine being in a state of oneness creating life out of darkness, often through sound. It is the most common type of creation myth and is found in cultures on all continents.[1] The Judeo-Christian creation story is an example of an infinite being creating life out of a void through the sound of the words 'Let there be light.' The big bang theory is based on a similar idea of an explosion of energy in the dark void of space creating early forms of life that evolved over time. In a Native Hawai'ian creation story, darkness contained a male and a female spirit who parented other beings, first in the sea and air and eventually onto land, when male Po-ne'e-aku (Night Leaving) and female Poeiemai (Night Pregnant) were born. They in turn gave birth to the dawn (that is, visible light) and to humans and the Earth as we know it.

Instead of demonising darkness with devils, Indigenous mythologies consider darkness the purest form of light, representing the womb of the cosmos from which all light emerges.[2] After all, white rejects or reflects all colours whereas black contains or absorbs them. But because of colonisation and mass migration, nearly every person on the planet has been exposed to a Western cosmology and has had to adapt and adopt some of it to survive. Indigenous peoples often describe this as 'living in two worlds'. In Western cosmology, to be human is to be the supreme species in a struggle for survival, and to be 'Indigenous' is a political identity based on blood lineage, race, culture and a history of oppression. In an Indigenous cosmology, to be human is based on relationships of sacred reciprocity specific to a person's culture, land, lineage and clan. Identity is relational, intertwined with place through kinship with humans and non-humans (often called 'totems'). We need to know who we are and learn to survive in both worlds, both cosmologies.

Indigenous people often feel so interconnected with their land that when it is neglected or desecrated in the outer physical reality, they experience pain in their inner realities of the mind, body and spirit. This is why being forced off our lands (by humans or weather) is so shattering because our entire cosmology, our whole worldview, is based on being in the right relationship with that place. The 'great rupture with the Mother' and 'break with the psychological womb' described in week 9 as a basis of Wetiko are in everyone's lineage these days. Have you thought about the Indigenous identities and creation myths hidden beneath modern political identities?

EXERCISE

Read the example of Anglo US man David Dean, who has unpacked the history of whiteness in his lineage.[3] Consider the cultures that make up your ancestry, using the definition of ancestry from week 6. What do you know about their creation myths? Make some notes about what you know, and then do a little research to learn something new about your blood ancestors and ancestors of land and spirit.

Trauma

WEEK BEGINNING: _____

SEASON: _____

Trauma's meaning, causes and methods of healing differ by culture and cosmology. In Western science, trauma is typically defined as profound wounding that damages a person's ability to trust in life and self, resulting in existential crises.[1] Trauma is encoded in brain pathways rooted in fear or terror, and disgust or aversion. Feeling fear is intended to protect us from life-threatening danger, so our nervous systems rev up and prepare for crisis. Trauma causes our nervous systems to activate stress hormones when danger isn't present, creating flashbacks, emotional volatility, strained relationships, retraumatising experiences and severe stress.[2] Primary trauma occurs for a person who directly experienced it, and secondary trauma occurs for family and friends. There's also intergenerational trauma. A typical Western healing approach is individual counselling, with some alternative approaches including other family members, or integrating art therapy, body work or eye movement desensitisation and reprocessing (EMDR).[3] The underlying idea is that by surviving trauma we can become more resilient individuals.

In Indigenous science, all disease including trauma is indicative of disruption in the natural order of humans' interactions with the spirit world. This includes failure to honour the spiritual realm and our ancestors, neglecting cultural rituals or religious ceremonies or losing faith in the Creator.[4] Where Western scientists seek cures for diseases and treatments for trauma, Indigenous scientists view trauma and diseases as potential gifts of healing that can offer important insights into how to live well and bring new wise leadership into a community. Where Western science views a personality or ego as the centre of an individual being, an Indigenous medicine person or 'shaman' views a person's eternal spirit as the centre of being. That is why the heart is at the centre of a medicine wheel, to remind us that we are connected to ourselves, each other and all of creation.

In Indigenous science, to try to make trauma go away through suppression, denial or taking drugs (legal or illegal) is denying an important spiritual initiation needed by an individual and their community.[5] Experiencing and healing trauma includes all our relations, human and non-human. Through my PhD studies on Indigenous scientific approaches to healing trauma (which included Indigenous healing ceremonies and apprenticeships as well as Western scientific research), I found four underlying causes of trauma in Indigenous science:

⊙   disconnection from the Earth
⊙   unhealed ancestral trauma
⊙   soul loss
⊙   shaman's illness.

Let's discuss soul loss and shaman's illness, since they may be new concepts so far in this book. In Indigenous science, traumatic experiences propel us into terror and dissociation, creating soul loss, meaning that we are no longer fully present in ordinary reality because parts of our spirit have split off, fled or gotten lost. 'Soul' is understood to mean 'consciousness'.[6] To live with soul loss means we are not consciously whole in the moment, that parts of us are frozen in an unresolved past, causing us to lose energy and feel disoriented, weak, anxious and depressed and to exhibit signs of mental and emotional illness. We may have internalised punishment or protectively hidden parts of ourselves that were unsafe to express, or internalised poisonous emotions like anger, bitterness, envy, fear, greed, hate, intolerance, pride, rage, resentment and vanity that need to be released).[7]

Our task as healers is to allow alchemy to occur so that sh*t we are carrying in our hearts, minds, bodies and spirits can instead turn into fertiliser for ourselves and others. By consciously choosing to move into fear and terror and aversion and disgust when we are in a safe space, we can reconnect with lost soul parts. In doing so we gain knowledge that expands our individual and collective understanding of ourselves and our world. This is seen as the sacred calling underlying a shaman's illness. Trauma is considered a spiritual offering of a huge amount of energy that can redirect us into a new identity like a phoenix rising out of ashes. Indigenous healers are called 'medicine people' or shamans because through healing trauma we embody medicine by living in a wiser way and offering support to others who are struggling through similar wounds.

We heal by consciously going into our traumatic states in a safe space. We are born being able to express few sounds, and similarly much of the traumatic energy of rebirthing ourselves is preverbal. Indigenous traumatic healing requires us to access profound, primal energies, to re-member ourselves by moving through layers of pain, and being with and expressing chaotic, violent, preconscious and unconscious energies through visions, bodily sensations and movements and dream-like states of consciousness outside of a Western cosmology.[8]

Trauma gives us the ability to enter into altered states of consciousness, and by transforming that gift from sh*tty triggered experiences of traumatic dissociation into a skilful powerful method of connecting with the ethereal, spiritual, sub- and un-conscious realms, we gain access to profound wisdom and aspects of life that others do not experience. Let's further explore skilful and healthy methods of dissociation or altering consciousness through the following exercise and further discussion in week 12.

EXERCISE

Reflect on a traumatic experience you have had. How did
it change your understanding of yourself? Your place in the
world? Of life itself? Now see if you can reflect on a deeper level
of consciousness through relaxing into a drum journey.[9]

Altered consciousness

WEEK BEGINNING: _____

SEASON: _____

Dissociation in Western science tends to be seen as a negative separation from ourselves, but in Indigenous science it can be a positive altering of everyday reality, allowing us to connect more deeply with the Creator. In fact, dissociating may be the 'single most widespread psycho-therapeutic technique in the world today'.[1] By altering our everyday consciousness, we can heal by re-membering lost soul parts and developing spiritual gifts to share in community. Drumming, as in the journey in week 11, is commonly used as a metaphor for the heartbeat, and rhythmic patterns of drumming, dancing, chanting or breathing help us get into a meditative or flow state of being. Prayer, meditation, sweating (with or without the inclusion of ice bathing), fasting, isolation in nature, ayahuasca[2] and similar psychotropic plants are other common tools Indigenous scientists use for altering consciousness.

When we alter our consciousness in communal ceremony, we empathically connect and can collectively pull each other deeper than we would be able to go alone. It is also a powerful way to connect with our ancestors and honour cultural rituals. In week 5 we reflected on ceremony, so I hope you already understand that there is a huge difference between a group of friends taking magic mushrooms at a night club and a group of people carefully collecting magic mushrooms in the wilderness and spending a night fasting and connecting to that land with fungal medicine through a sacred ceremony.

A problem with modern spiritual materialism is attempting to do ceremony out of its Indigenous context. Plant and fungal medicines have deeper relationships with their indigenous lands and ecosystems. We may experience healing through an ayahuasca ceremony in New York City, but it will not be as safe, centred or powerful as healing with ayahuasca in the jungles of the Amazon where her spirit is grounded with Indigenous people who have been working with her for thousands of years.

It is important to consider intentions and tools we use for altering consciousness, as well as the underlying cosmology of a ceremony. I have experienced group meditations based on Buddhist and Hindu cosmologies where we meditated through our inner or third eye and sent energy towards the ceiling. While interesting, I do not find such experiences grounding or centring, and I do not choose to repeat them. Tools intended to help us embody ourselves more fully, not just cleanse our inner vision or quiet our minds, support healing across the entire medicine wheel.

EXERCISE

Take a moment to reflect on where your energy is right now: are you in your head a bit while reading this? Take a break with a guided body relaxation meditation[3] and notice where your energy is and how centred and grounded you feel.

When we eat, we can only take in so much food in one sitting, from chewing to digesting and releasing. It's the same with information. Indigenous science is about fully embodying our knowledge and integrating it into our lives. In Western science people talk about processing information, but often that's understood to be top-down, taken in through our heads. For example, we may realise that we have been dehydrated lately so we set phone alarm reminders throughout the day to drink water. While this may practically help, it will not get to the root of the issue. Were we in our heads so much that we lost touch with our feelings and were unaware when we were thirsty? Was this because we felt unsafe or were behaving manically?

This is why many Western medical treatments are criticised as symptom management rather than healing. Healing requires that we gain a deeper understanding of the patterns we are in, and it enables us to experience renewed inner motivation and insight into new ways of being that are healthier. When we are focused on bettering our relationship with water and what it means to us, it takes more work than simply setting an alarm. We may meditate on water and nourishment, put water on our altar or give an offering to a nearby pond to honour how water keeps us alive. (This doesn't mean you don't set an alarm to help yourself out physically; it just means you don't stop there.) A healing process cannot be forced to conform to a timeline; healing emerges from the darkness of the Unknown, like all of creation. It requires us to ask questions and await insights, signs and messages from the universe, and continually take steps in an iterative process.

For example, I had serious digestive issues when I was younger, and for nearly 15 years I could not eat wheat, among other things. I avoided it, took supplements to strengthen my digestive system and put an image of wheat on my altar. One day I woke up and felt it was safe to eat bread. My husband thought I was crazy, but it worked, and I have been able to eat wheat since that day, though Western doctors told me I'd have to avoid it the rest of my life. Good thing I never believed them and remained open to (without expecting) healing.

Altered consciousness work is typically done as ritual or ceremony, which begin with cleansing. Cleansing and purification are often done with smoke or smudging. Smoke symbolises cleansing of space for healing and is intended to remind us of the sacredness of life. Plants vary by culture and place, such as Native American tobacco, cedar, sweetgrass or sage, palo santo in the Amazon or Aboriginal Australian acacia and eucalypt.[4] (Please be mindful that some plants like sage are being overharvested due to spiritual materialism, making Indigenous communities less able to use them.)

Whether we smoke or smudge, spray a liquid like rosewater, take a spiritual bath or do another ritual, once we have cleansed ourselves and our space, we become more receptive to receiving. A cleansing ritual may be as mundane as setting a table with gratitude before nourishing ourselves with a meal, or as profound as fasting in the wilderness for a vision quest. Altering consciousness can be subtle, such as experiencing a bit more space to appreciate the aroma of a meal, or it can be a big bang of suddenly seeing psychedelic images. These extremes, and everything in between, offer different opportunities for growth and healing.

EXERCISE

Print or draw two versions of the medicine wheel exercise from week 2. In one, focus on cleansing: what helps your body, spirit, mind and emotions cleanse and be clear and flowing? In the other, focus on nourishment. Then take time this week to cleanse and nourish yourself and your space (inside and out).

WEEK

13

The Unknown

WEEK BEGINNING: _____

SEASON: _____

These days we are so used to being able to quickly 'know' something that when we can't remember we immediately look it up online, and if we can't find an answer, our minds may fixate on 'needing to know' in an addictive way that's challenging. Some ways of thinking, such as mathematics, can trick us into thinking there is one answer: surely 2 + 2 = 4, right? Well, that's only 'true' when we use a numerical system in base 10. If you think about the system for telling time in base 12, 2 am + 2 pm does not equal 4 pm! And mathematics includes plenty of wacky things like imaginary and irrational numbers. So if you are thinking that in mathematics there is one objectively 'right answer', you are focusing on a certain kind of maths, like focusing on bright stars in the sky instead of the whole canvas of brighter and darker spaces.

In week 12 we mentioned that creation comes from the darkness of the Unknown into the known – that classic phrase about coming from darkness into light. But this is where English is a bit limited as a language, because a dichotomy of darkness and light is too dualistic and simplistic for Indigenous science. In fact, in Indigenous science creation stories, darkness is the purest form of light, the womb of the cosmos from which all light emerges.[1] You may find it helpful to remember that black absorbs and white reflects visible light. In week 9 we mentioned that many Indigenous cultures have constellations in the darkness of the Milky Way, and in Indigenous science in general there is an understanding that the Earth and the Sky are reflections of each other, including brighter and darker aspects.

EXERCISE

Let's take a moment to unpack the concepts of 'mystery', 'darkness' and the 'Unknown'. Make three columns on a piece of paper and write each word in one of the columns. Take a minute and in a stream of consciousness way, without thinking carefully, write feelings and thoughts you associate with each concept. Then take a moment to reflect on where these associations came from, and if you want to let any go.

MYSTERY   DARKNESS   UNKNOWN

Now that you are more aware of some of your underlying biases it will be easier to talk about the Unknown. In general, what we don't know feels scary. We all have different approaches to facing fears, but it is generally easier to walk into a scary situation rather than run into it with scissors. In terms of metaphorically walking into the Unknown, you do it all the time. As a child, nearly everything you learned was a pioneering effort into the Unknown. For example, you likely learned that if you do not watch where you walk, you may trip and fall, but if you only watch the ground, you may bump your head instead. The same applies to exploring the Unknown of our inner worlds. You may be having some hard feelings and decide to share them with a close friend. Your friend may ask some reflective questions that help you understand yourself better, or they may get triggered that you brought up hard feelings, leaving you feeling abandoned and attacked. If you are later able to talk about what happened and both take responsibility, you may learn that even when you trigger your friend, you can trust them to self-reflect and reconnect. Or you may learn that a topic is too hard for your friend to help you with, so you respect their limits and share those feelings with someone else. When we are dealing with the Unknown, it helps to give grace, limit expectations and accept that learning processes are messy.

So what does it reflect about Western culture that constellations and the traditional stories about them are only based on the bright lights? By focusing on the bright lights we feel we can 'know' by naming them and labelling their paths, we are obscuring the majority of what we see in the night sky: darkness. Creation stories and their teachings are the foundation of a cosmology and all the cultures arising from it. In Judeo-Christian creation stories, the darkness is typically demonised by devils and fallen angels and many children learn to be afraid of the dark. Yet in some Indigenous cultures, to be able to run through a forest in the dark was a practice to develop your clair senses, and your trust in the darkness and in your country. And in many Indigenous North American cultures, instead of 'God' or 'Oneness', people refer to the 'Great Mystery' as an energy that connects all beings.

Mysteries may or may not be scary. There is an exciting aspect to mystery stories in Western culture because we expect they will be 'solved' at the end, and we await a resolution of tension. But in life, the essence of a mystery is not that we solve it, but that we allow it to be unknown and see if any insight emerges as we sit in that unknown space. This requires us to use an 'I don't know' mind. When I have an I don't know mind, I feel humble and receptive to learning. I have faith that I cannot know everything, or even know all that much, and that what I need to know will arise in my life at the right time.

An I don't know state of mind feels very freeing. We don't feel like we *should* have the answers to problems, or even that something painful is necessarily a problem. It is really helpful with spiritual questions like 'Why did this happen to me?' That question makes us feel victimised, and tends to attract people to us who validate our 'poor me' story, fuelling further feelings of helplessness and resentment in a downward spiral. Instead, if we think to ourselves that tough things happen to everyone, human and non-human, so 'Why not me?', we find it easier to accept an experience and seek support that empowers us to move forward.

When we don't expect to know something it takes pressure off our minds to make sense of things beyond the mind's capacity and allows us to feel more peace. In an Indigenous cosmology, we trust that some forces of nature are greater than us humans and we see absolute or objective certainty as dangerous, leading to denial and fanaticism. Even with knowledge we feel highly confident about, we retain a little doubt. The only certainty is uncertainty, and the only constant is change. We trust that life is here for us and by taking time to connect with the Unknown, we receive insight when we need it.

EXERCISE

Find a mirror. You may wish to be alone or to whisper if others are around. Looking at your reflection, say the following or something similar that comes to you: *'I do not know why. I do not know how. I do not know when. I do not know who I am. I allow my mind to trust the process of life as it unfolds and let go of my need to know. From now on I honour the Unknown.'*

Take a moment to go within and observe how you feel. Set an intention to have an I don't know state of mind throughout the next week, and notice how it changes your interactions and inner voice.

WEEK

14

Flow and shadow

WEEK BEGINNING: _____

SEASON: _____

We often call something random if it happened unexpectedly yet in seeming synchronicity. The word 'random' in English can be traced back to the word 'Rhine' (the river in Germany), referring to a river's natural flow that perfectly weaves through the land linking other bodies of water and bringing nourishment to the country and its inhabitants. So next time you hear someone say 'That was random!', maybe like me you will smile to yourself that what they meant was 'That was flow!'

In week 12 we talked about 'flow' as a state of consciousness where we experience oneness and ease, where life seems to unfold pretty effortlessly and we feel part of something bigger than ourselves. When we are able to accept the moment, we trust life and are along for the ride . . . But we are human, and part of our journey is that we do not sit in that flow state 24/7, if we sit in that state of consciousness much at all. We each carry traumas and other wounds that cause us to reject reality and project our fears into situations and onto people who may or may not be able to help us heal.

When we make space for the Unknown, we make space for flow. When we live in obligations, expectations and keeping up appearances, we tend to feel dead inside and miss opportunities for growth and healing. I see a lot of confusion about flow in New-Age thinking about manifestation. A lot of people try to force a dream into being, cling to a specific vision, and push through Indigenous science data suggesting alterations to the vision or alternative paths that might be more supportive. It's the difference between being a forceful, controlling, rigid top-down dictator and a powerful, trusting, open-minded ground-up co-creator. As co-creators (or co-dreamers), we acknowledge that we are not in control of *how* a dream might come into being – we trust that life wants what's best for us and have faith that our dreams are realisable. We may not know *why* we have a dream, *where* it came from or *who* will support it. We may only have a vague sense of *what* the dream is, because we know it needs to evolve within a context much bigger than our minds can comprehend. So we willingly walk into the Unknown to facilitate our dreams to grow.

Using our I don't know mind is key to being in flow. What blocks us from flow are wounds, traumas and shadows. 'Shadow' was an idea popularised by Carl Jung that he defined as the 'dark side' of a personality, the aspects of self that a person doesn't identify with, projects onto others and reacts to. If you think about how shadows work in the physical world, the shape and even existence of a shadow is entirely dependent on the angle and strength of light shining on a physical form. A tree that provides great shade at 4 pm may provide none at all at noon. (Interestingly, some languages like Spanish do not have separate terms for 'shade' and 'shadow'.) So the concept of a shadow, like all of Indigenous science, is relative, not absolute. With practise we can get better at seeing our shadows and understanding their forms in different contexts.

It is foolish to expect to 'know' or see our shadows fully, as shadows, like every other aspect of life, are part of the Great Mystery. Still, there are three main ways we can become more aware of our shadows. The first is to pay attention to the blocks in flow in your life. When we first start to do that it can seem quite daunting, like there are blocks everywhere. That's okay. Having awareness about where we experience flow, and where we struggle, empowers us to prioritise our focus of growth and healing. We humans are meant to have limits and growing edges, places where we feel free and flowing, and spaces where we feel blocked, stuck, lost and overwhelmed. That's the journey we're all on. One way to start practising being in flow and seeing how it feels is by doing the exercise opposite.

EXERCISE

Create flow time by carving out space in your schedule to spontaneously be in the moment, meaning that you have no plans or agendas. Begin by relaxing, grounding and centring yourself, then allowing yourself to instinctively do what organically comes to you. You may say to yourself 'Legs, take me somewhere!' then go for a walk and be surprised where you end up. You may do familiar things in a different way. If you do this for a few weeks, notice how you feel about going with the flow in life, about accepting the unexpected and trusting yourself to navigate the Unknown.

The second way to see our shadows more clearly is to learn from others. Just like we can see the outline of a friend's shadow in a way they can't see it themselves because of our perspective, we can learn from people we trust who know us well, and from wise people who are able to offer a clear reflection that resonates within our hearts and rings with truth. We can learn a lot from non-humans too; for example, many of us have learned that capitalism is unsustainable, and that systemic change is needed to slow climate change and mass extinctions.

And a third way to learn about our shadows is by illuminating collective cultural shadows through encounters with people from other cultures. For example, some Western scientific studies have found that the placebo effect has been strengthening over time in the US.[1] One possible explanation is that for-profit drug companies directly advertise to consumers in the US. People from outside the US see this huge collective shadow when they first encounter advertisements on television saying 'If you suffer from sleeplessness, talk to your doctor about how Chlorigil[2] can help.' Another explanation may be that the collective ritual of taking a pill to feel better has, for many people, become a belief that pills lead to feeling better, so their minds create that reality even with placebos.

EXERCISE

Centre and ground yourself first. Then sit at a keyboard or with a pen and paper (or a voice recorder if you find it easier to speak than write), and in a stream of consciousness, respond to the following: 'I believe . . . .'

Did any of your beliefs surprise you? Does it feel like something is missing?

Belief is a powerful tool, and being aware of our beliefs can help us navigate shadows. For example, I believe Western medicine is designed for physical crisis and avoid it otherwise, but my husband believes Western medicine is helpful for a variety of issues. If you think about it like a Venn diagram (a system of overlapping circles that show the relationships between things), our beliefs have a pretty small area of overlap. This means we can't fully support each other in that aspect of our lives. This shadow awareness helps us limit expectations of each other, know when to seek support from others, and gives us a heads-up about when we may be asking something tough or triggering of each other.

WEEK

15

Faith

WEEK BEGINNING: _____

SEASON: _____

Common phrases about faith are 'faith based', referring primarily to evangelical Christians, 'blind faith', referring to faith being invisible, which is also in Christianity, and 'a leap of faith', referring to going into the Unknown hoping for a better situation. I will clarify how I see faith and how it differs from trust and hope, and hopefully that will clarify the concepts for you too. The quote that rings truest to me about faith comes from shamanic practitioner Christina Pratt: 'Faith is freefall. It is the liquid state of grace in which all change is possible. Without faith we are unable to cross that gap between what was and what needs to be.'[1] Words that relate closely for me are 'reliance' and 'belief'. When I realise that the fear I feel is existential and not due to being in imminent danger, I lean into faith and practices that support me to maintain and heal it, to experience something different that I clair 'know' is possible.

Our relationship with faith and willingness to lean into that loss of control, that liquid state of flow, has a huge impact on our lives. Placing my faith in the belief that 'Family always takes care of each other' set me up for existential crisis when someone in my family neglected or betrayed me. Placing my faith in the belief 'Family always tries to take care of each other' means I still feel hurt, but with less existential crisis that my faith was placed in an idea that was experientially shown to me to be untrue. And instead, placing my faith in the belief that 'Whatever I need comes to me when I need it' takes the pressure off expecting family members to show up for me and creates more space for a friend, neighbour or even stranger to help me when I need it.

I have found that blind faith leads us to being let down, and even lose faith in faith itself. Through culture, family and life experiences, we learn to place our faith without conscious awareness. It is through being challenged in our beliefs, realising things we took as 'truth' are not in fact true, that we are called on to question our beliefs and reassess where we consciously place our faith. In this way, a healthy, spiritual adult's relationship with faith is grown through an iterative process. We place faith in something, then we see how it feels to live with that. Placing faith in the universe always supporting me has felt very healing. I've found that even when tough things come up, I see the value of letting go and making space for better support and connection to emerge. Placing faith in life always being there for me also ensures that I limit identification as a victim. If I am victimised, I do not let that pain reach an existential level. In this way, faith supports me to gracefully navigate the Unknown.

Where faith relates to interactions with the Unknown, trust relates to truths that we can rely on, that we 'know', such as trusting that the sun will set tonight and rise tomorrow. The Russian proverb 'Trust but verify' famously used by Ronald Reagan reflects a lack of faith and trust. It really says: 'I don't trust you, but I am willing to be shown that I can.' Growing up, I was unsafe, because I was being abused. When I moved out on my own, I dared to hope that life could be better, and I took a leap of faith by deciding to try believing that life was always for my benefit and there was a positive purpose to the pain I'd been through. At first it was just an idea inspired in part by Louise Hay's *You Can Heal Your Life* (Hay House, 1985), but then I started to experience it. And when my faith was challenged, I was still able to have faith in life being for my benefit because I learned the limits of my personal power, and the nature of certain situations as dangers that I needed boundaries and protection from.

The idea that if a character trait isn't present we can just 'manifest it' is a trick, and the idea that if it isn't there it never will be and we better accept that and take a pill to replace it is also a trick. They're both stuck in dualistic thinking. A belief that we need a pill can prevent healing, but not taking a pill that would support our current survival may be dangerous. It's important to discern when we are and aren't helpless. And discernment is strengthened by building trust, with ourselves first and foremost. By following through on my words with actions – even little agreements I make with myself – I become a more trustworthy person and improve my discernment abilities.

All beliefs create biases, blind spots and shadows. Believing that life is always there for me has predisposed me to move into some trauma and pain that I might have avoided if I had already had more discernment. I've chosen to place faith in my journey being worthwhile, warts and all, and the process of gaining discernment being a messy one. It seems to me that we humans are not as powerful as we often claim (like blaming ourselves entirely for climate change), nor as powerless as we often feel (like when we're in a job or relationship that isn't working and feel unable to make a change).

When we feel powerless, we often turn to personal egoic desires and hopes that things will change, which may lead to denial. I have found that the best way to use hope is to express wishes and desires without expectation or attachment to result. This way we learn what is true, and what we hope to be true. Re-engaging in a relationship with an alcoholic with the hope that this time it will be different can show us where we are in denial and improve our discernment. Acceptance of such misplaced hope helps us learn the limits of our sphere of influence and individual responsibility. It then becomes clearer where we need to cut our losses and take a leap of faith into the Unknown.

The biggest block I find in most of us to flowing with faith and trust is shame and low self-worth beliefs. This often results in dualistic flipping between optimistic and cynical beliefs, such as 'People are trustworthy' to 'I can't trust anybody' rather than navigating the more nuanced reality 'Some people are trustworthy sometimes.' I don't want to entirely put down the practice of affirmations, because they can be truly empowering. But it is important to understand that you can't sit in front of a crocodile and continually affirm that you are safe and expect you will remain safe. Because that crocodile has its own nature, and its desire and ability to attack and eat you is dangerous to your survival. You are not in control of this co-created relationship dynamic of predator and prey.

Sometimes with people we have a hard time realising we are sitting with crocodiles – like there's a belief in many workplaces that everyone will collaborate because we are all on the same team. No, we are not. Every person has individual desires and needs in addition to being part of a team, and when in conflict, most people will choose what feels like maintaining their personal survival over self-sacrifice for the team. (That's understandable, considering most people are individually hired into 'teams' of people they haven't met before, and being fired can threaten their physical survival.)

EXERCISE

Read the article by Brianna Wiest about relationships and self-worth.[2] Reflect on relationships in your life that feel imbalanced, on relational dynamics that nourish and deplete you. Where are you making sacrifices and compromises, or martyring yourself? Reflect on beliefs underlying these dynamics.

WEEK

16

Survival strategies

WEEK BEGINNING: _____

SEASON: _____

In Chief Seattle's famous speech, he said the way US settlers were treating Mother Earth was moving us from 'The end of living [into] the beginning of survival.'[1] As you know, across the planet species are going extinct, human languages and cultures are dying, polar ice caps are melting, and sacred lands are disappearing underwater. Many of us understandably feel overwhelmed by the depth of pain on the planet right now, by how many systems we are caught up in that feel *wrong*. If we numb ourselves with substances, live in our heads or create righteous and secure bubbles around ourselves, we are disconnecting. Accepting reality as it is, however painful, allows us to experience wholeness and peace. This helps us become heart-centred warriors who bring healing medicine into the world. Being centred and grounded allows us to clarify what our personal responsibilities are and what we have power to change and influence. We can live our values without judging or blaming others who are bypassing their pain through denial or numbness.

In order to do this, we must first release the tremendous burden of having to 'fix' and better the world. It might sound crazy because things that feel wrong are happening. But in a holistic, Indigenous cosmology we need to hold that paradox. In order to heal from child sexual abuse, I needed to accept that though I do not understand why, as a collective, we humans have not yet learned that child sexual abuse is wrong and deeply damaging and therefore found ways to organise ourselves to prevent it. I also do not understand why we are collectively destroying Mother Earth, our lifeblood and basis for survival. I have some ideas why, but on a deep level I do not 'know'.

Allowing self-destruction to be something we humans are learning feels heartbreaking. Something that helped me accept this reality was hearing from the Hopi people of the south-western US (and later from other Indigenous cultures) that in their lore humans have already destroyed the world a number of times. Their acceptance of this lesson as part of the survival struggle of human nature helped me let go of clinging to this Earth as the only one. The law from Western science in physics that no energy can be created or destroyed says this also: that even when we physically lose a species or landform, those energies somehow transform and continue to exist. Many species that are long extinct live on in spirit, and many of us seem to enjoy digging up their bones, learning about the Earth's past and imagining them walking around. Part of this paradox is that such destruction feels quite devastating, and we do need to honour those feelings, be with the grief, potentially make some changes within our own lives and advocate for large-scale social change. Some aspects of life are quite brutal.

There is a common New-Age misconception that all energy can be 'transformed into light', into something less brutal. But this denies the nature of some primal energies. If you have ever locked eyes with a crocodile or bear you have likely felt chilled inside and known that you were not at the top of the food chain. If you have ever been in a warzone, witnessed someone being killed or experienced a trauma such as sexual violence, you have endured some brutality. It is a hard energy for most of us to be with, yet other animals seem to flow in and out of it with more ease. Your house cat may mew at you with big eyes one minute, and the next viciously attack a bird and rip open its guts for entertainment. Such is nature, including *our* human nature. We carry brutal, primal survival energy too. Have you experienced fiercely protective feelings for a child? Have you fiercely fought off an attack physically, verbally or otherwise? Have you killed another animal?

Survival strategies are fundamental, primal coping mechanisms intended to keep us alive. We all have many of them, and they differ by situation. If you think about plants and animals, you can see what works differs by a being's nature and environment. For example, a mouse can much more easily avoid a predator by scurrying and hiding under a rock than a skunk, so the skunk uses a different tactic of trying to stink bomb its way out of becoming prey. The common survival strategies we learn about are fighting, fleeing and freezing. Recently, 'fawning' has been added, referring to appeasing someone to survive. Western psychologist Paul Valent suggested the following survival strategies instead: rescuing/attaching, adapting/asserting, fighting/fleeing and competing/co-operating.[2] Valent's research found links between the strategies within these four groupings, like a spectrum of behaviour and a push-pull tension between what we do and what we attract.

For example, if you are being a victim, you may attract someone who wants to rescue you and be the saviour. Yet sometimes we are in trouble and need rescuing, and it can be healing for someone to save us from pain that they weren't saved from experiencing. Please set an intention to release any judgement you have about survival strategies. Nature does not judge a tiger as a worse creature for mauling a pig to survive than a bird for pecking at seeds. A horse has more physical impact walking on the ground than an ant. Mother Earth supports us all to survive regardless of our differences. Awareness about how we are surviving in different areas of our lives can be empowering. For example, knowing that you tend to keep quiet about conflict at work means you need to be in an environment mostly aligning with your values to avoid feeling abused or burnt out. And teaching your friend that you are an introvert who freezes when emotionally overwhelmed means they're less likely to worry about your silence and more likely to give you some space and wait for you to get back into contact.

If you do not feel good about some of your survival strategies, I suggest first accepting where you're at and focusing on having faith that you're doing your best. Survival fears trigger us so deeply, and it takes time to rebalance ourselves. Sometimes we need to experience different aspects of a survival strategy in order to heal trauma and wounding. For example, if you were emotionally abused as a child and attached to your parental abuser to survive, as an adult you may need to rescue yourself from an abusive relationship to heal that wound and shift your survival strategy. It can help to reflect on survival strategies you were taught, if you were culturally or socially expected to behave in certain ways that you no longer need to or whether, like a horse or ant, some are simply in your nature. Knowing our nature brings peace and self-acceptance, even if it can't be changed.

EXERCISE

Set an intention to become aware of survival strategies you and those close to you tend to use. Observe behaviours for a few days. Notice when, where and with whom you feel your survival threatened so that you go into a survival strategy. Notice how you feel when using different strategies. Reflect on where they came from, whether they feel more natural or learned. Ask yourself intuitively if it is possible to change any survival strategies you don't like. Practise acceptance.

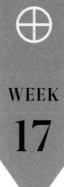

WEEK

17

Birth and rebirth

WEEK BEGINNING: _____

SEASON: _____

Earth's cycle embedded within the medicine wheel is birthing → living → dying → rebirthing. When we think about birth, the first images that come to mind are likely a mother and baby. But what nourishes the baby in the womb is the placenta, and after the baby is born it continues to provide nourishment through the umbilical cord and is birthed soon after. The placenta is thus our primal nourisher, and Indigenous scientists around the world have practices to honour and offer it to the Earth.

EXERCISE

Do online image searches for 'placenta' and 'placenta print'. Notice how the placenta print looks like an archetypal image: the tree of life.

Many Aboriginal Australians see the placenta as your hologram providing a map or guide for your life.[1] It is ceremonially buried in the Earth to provide direction for you once you reach puberty, when the earth-bound knowledge you need is awakened by your first drops of menstrual blood or semen that touch the ground.[2] The Diné (also known as the Navajo) similarly bury the placenta in sacred ancestral ground so tribal members grow up with a strong cultural identity.[3] The Māori have this practice so strongly embedded within their culture that their word for 'land' and 'placenta' is the same.[4] In the Hmong culture in Laos, your spirit is believed to be doomed wandering the Earth unable to join the ancestors in the spirit world unless you can return to the place your placenta was buried and reunite with it.[5] In Korea and China, many people burn the placenta and keep some ashes to sprinkle into their food to nourish them when they are sick.[6] In parts of Indonesia your placenta is considered to be your older sibling or twin;[7] in Iceland it is your guardian angel.[8] In Africa, the Ibo people treat the placenta as a dead twin and give it full burial rites,[9] while the Baganda people see it as your 'double' with its own spirit residing in the umbilical cord.[10]

Wuradjuri scientist Minmia explains the sacred reciprocity of burying the placenta: 'The placenta is extremely rich so it nourishes [Mother Earth]. The Earth needs nourishment as much as we need nourishment. It is a two-way thing. It also honours the Earth by placing responsibility for the child's journey in her.'[11] And yet in modern hospitals multiple placentas are incinerated together. Minmia says, 'because it's melted together it carries the print of other [people's spirits] with which it was burnt – so there's confusion . . . Rebirthing can repair this.[12] In Western science, if the umbilical cord is cut while still pumping the baby loses blood volume, but Minmia says 'it is like spiritually blinding our babies' because those final minutes spiritually provide the baby with 'its seeds of instruction – how to follow the [placental] map.'[13]

Most of us were born in a hospital and our placentas were not ceremonially honoured, though Indigenous scientists teach us that it is vitally important to do so. We can do rebirthing ceremonies to heal and reclaim our innate connection with Mother Earth so that we experience grounding, safety, reciprocity and guidance. I encourage you to think about all aspects of Earth's cycle (birthing → living → dying → rebirthing) as processes, not specific moments. For example, dying is a process of our bodies shutting down, disconnecting with our souls/spirits, then decaying into the ground. Similarly, there is a moment when we are physically born out of our mother's womb, then so many moments when we are born psychologically, emotionally, spiritually and physically as we grow and move through our lives.

EXERCISE

Ask your parents about your birth, what they remember feeling and experiencing. Consider also doing a drum journey (you can find one at https://www.youtube.com/watch?v=1Bk1oCmcuqQ) with the intention of gaining insight into what you felt and the projections people made onto baby you at birth.

There are many ways to do rebirthing ceremonies. Some cultures traditionally bury placentas at the family home, others choose a type of tree to bury the placenta under to connect the qualities of that tree with the person and some have specific ancestral burial grounds. Do what feels best to you. If you are unsure, you can place a power object on your ancestral altar and ask for insight about a rebirthing ceremony then await guidance through dreams, visions, clair senses and other signs. You could also just do a ceremony, and if you don't experience much shifting in your life in the following weeks, you could do another ceremony once you get more insight into what would work better. There's no need to place pressure on ceremonies being 'right', because as long as we do something with sacred intention and authentic action, we can await feedback and lived experience wisdom to see how well it's working. In all areas of life, including ceremony, please allow yourself to work within an iterative learning process as you reclaim Indigenous science processes and knowledge.

EXERCISE

Set an intention to do a rebirthing ceremony. Find an object like a rock, or draw a picture of your symbolic placenta. Choose a place that feels safe and nourishing to give your placenta to the Earth. Dig a small hole with your hands or a stick and place your symbolic placenta in the hole, along with your DNA such as hair, blood and skin. Then take a bit of earth and rub it into your belly button to honour your new umbilical cord connection. Tell the Earth you are committed to being in sacred reciprocity with Her and will take care of Her, and in return ask that She support you and offer you guidance, insight, grounding and healing. Sit mindfully and meditatively in this spot for a while and see what thoughts and feelings emerge.

You may from now on celebrate this day as your spiritual birthday or rebirthday, and return to feel nourished and ask for insight about your earthly journey.

WEEK

18

Death and decay

WEEK BEGINNING: _____

SEASON: _____

When we think about death, many of us imagine the moment someone's spirit or soul leaves their physical body. In Indigenous science death is considered a process of decaying and dying across any and all areas of the medicine wheel. Such processes often trigger fear of the Unknown and intense emotion and are big opportunities for letting go and transforming. Imagine a rotting tree. Your mind might label such a tree 'dead', but in Indigenous science, while the tree is in the process of decaying and dying it provides a home to many birds, insects and critters, as well as fodder for fungi, mosses and moulds among others. When we look at decaying and dying as a process of transformation, we can see it as a beautiful and important phase of Earth's cycle of birth → life → death → rebirth. You can't have a rebirth without a death!

In week 11 on trauma we introduced the shaman's illness, a traumatic ego death and initiation in the form of a spiritual crisis. Decaying and dying, through a shaman's illness or any spiritual initiation, takes time. Usually people experience it as an iterative process, with some aspects of their lives falling apart and needing to be let go, some rebirthing with life looking different than it used to, other aspects falling apart and more being reborn. All spiritual initiations are death → rebirth processes. They are designed such that the fiery nature of Spirit breaks us down and reforges us anew.

Such processes necessarily include trauma, as all deaths and births are traumatic experiences. It is through trauma and ordeal that we are tested and have the biggest opportunities to grow. Anyone who has witnessed childbirth knows that birthing is a traumatic process, and dying is as well, though our experiences of the intensity of such transformations vary. Traumatic experiences in general compel the heart to unfold, expose new vulnerabilities within us and create opportunities for growing, learning and building strength and resilience.

Through trauma we often experience an intense loss of control and a state of existential crisis where our foundational understandings of the world and ourselves are challenged. We also gain insight and a new view of life, but seeing the world in ways outside social norms can be challenging. We may become sensitive to feelings and experiences that other people are blocking or numb to, triggering in us feelings of rejection, social and cultural alienation, doubt, fear, shame, grief, confusion and anger. The following tend to bring ease during such a journey: faith in something bigger or more powerful than us; trusting the process as a natural part of life; giving ourselves the grace to experience unpleasant change and for life to be chaotic; paying attention to Indigenous science data, including dreams, synchronicities, signs, patterns and symbols; and finding ways to express hard, painful thoughts and emotions and to ground intense energies.

Whether through spiritual initiation or otherwise, we all experience death and decay. When we think about a tree decaying we don't imagine it would ever resist such a process, but we humans often *do* resist it, making it much harder for ourselves and others. What we suppress, avoid and reject remains in our lives in some form until we accept it. Most of us survive our childhoods by suppressing, avoiding and rejecting quite a lot. When we fly the nest, we begin to pick through the mess we've inherited to learn who we are and how to live our values. If we avoid expressing some anger and setting a boundary and instead carry the energy as resentment, we may feel victimised and carry some pain in our bellies. If we don't speak our truth, we may feel silenced and get a throat infection. And when we are rejecting and suppressing a number of different things, we experience a jumble of patterns that require patience and determination to unpack, express, let go and heal.

When looking at death and decay, consider the entire medicine wheel. For example, a mental death could be realising that assuming people are doing their best feels better than assuming people are intending to hurt us, even when their best is not impressive. Noticing old habits of thinking and allowing them to dissipate takes time. An emotional death might come through experiencing narcissistic abuse. The pain of a relationship may build to a point where we seek help and gain insight into behavioural patterns and cycles and learn how we are getting caught up in or enabling the pain to continue. A spiritual death may occur through an initiation, a near-death experience or use of psychedelics, so that afterwards we have a new understanding of the world and see things we didn't before. A physical death may be leaving your body through trauma. It could also be breaking up with a long-term partner, losing a job, house, pet or friend, or having a grown child move out.

EXERCISE

How do you feel when you reflect on death and decay? What aspects of your life are currently in a cycle of death and decay mentally? Emotionally? Spiritually? Physically? How do you tend to express or resist this energy?

In many cultures, death ceremonies are annual traditions, often taking place in autumn at harvest time. Most death ceremonies honour ancestors, and some include practices for your own death such as coffin ceremonies.[1] Most commonly known are Meso-America's Day of the Dead and the Celtic ceremony of Samhain or All Hallows' Eve.[2] In the majority of cultures, there are funeral ceremonies following a physical death, and in many cultures a year or so afterwards is a ceremony to honour the person becoming an ancestor and completing their journey to the Spirit world.

EXERCISE

Practise a death meditation such as imagining yourself
lying in a grave underground and your body decaying and
being eaten by worms, a guided one about your funeral[3] or a
guided one about your physical death.[4] How did it feel?

A prayer attributed to Native American cultures is 'Today is a good day to die.' It might sound macabre to start the day with such a prayer, but imagine what it would be like to live so fully with joy and presence, being with loved ones and doing what matters to you, that you feel at peace about each day being your last day on Earth. Imagine feeling that you have no unfinished business, no indebtedness, no overwhelming sense of 'having to' fulfil certain dreams or desires, or 'should-ing' yourself to do things you don't want to. Imagine letting it all go – this is a death practice. Such practices can be very freeing and help us feel balanced in a world where we are encouraged to chase desires, work towards goals, accumulate things and 'be good people' (which is often an expectation of self-suppression).

EXERCISE

Reflect on whether today is a good day to die. If not, why not?
What are you attached to? What could you let go of and/or change
about your life to feel at peace if this is your last day on Earth?

Synchronicity

WEEK BEGINNING: _____

SEASON: _____

In Indigenous science, timing is synchronicity. There are certain conditions that need to be met before a caterpillar will go into a cocoon, and before it will emerge as a butterfly. There is a season for each flowering plant to bud, fruit and go to seed; a season when birds build nests and lay eggs, aligning with baby snakes emerging from their eggs ready to eat fallen baby birds. The same is true for us humans and the synchronicity of our nature. As children we may play house and take care of younger siblings, but not until we are older are we able to become parents of our own babies. When we control environments and natural cycles, it takes us out of tune with our nature. It's as if all of our earthly non-human relatives are flowing in a symphonic dance and only we humans are moving out of step and singing out of key.

Being aware of where in our lives we feel in or out of sync with natural seasons and cycles is empowering. For example, many of us struggle to get to sleep at night with bright indoor lights overactivating cortisol and adrenaline, but if we spend time in the wilderness camping by a fire under starlight our melatonin kicks in and our sleep cycle reregulates. Similarly, eating seasonal fruits and vegetables feels better as it helps us be in sync with our non-human relatives and the Earth's cycle.

You can't force a caterpillar to become a butterfly or a flower to go from bud to bloom, so why do we force ourselves and our environments to be out of alignment with our nature? One simple thing to do is practise accepting what is with an intention of making minimal adjustments for your well-being and comfort. If you're cold, be cold and get a jumper if needed, and if you're old, be wrinkled and proud to project wisdom with your face! Every adjustment we make to our nature – whether taking a pill to prevent pregnancy or sealing off our houses to use air-conditioning – separates us from the rest of creation. It doesn't mean those choices are wrong, but it's empowering to be aware of when and why we make them. The essence of the word 'synchronicity' is that we are in sync with the Earth's cycle, so that even moving through death and decay and other tough stuff feels pretty effortless to accept and go with the flow.

For most of us it's not feasible to live as gently as our ancestors who altered their environments minimally and used fewer resources than we do.

But there are ways to live *more* simply and gently, helping us experience less separation. For instance, having a salt lamp next to my computer balances the positive ions emitted by the screen and brings me ease, and its fiery glow is comforting. Low, warm lighting throughout my house helps my body know it's night time, even though I'm inside. Having the windows open allows me to feel the temperature and hear the sounds from my environment and, since I live in the countryside, helps me be in sync with the seasons, weather and time of day. When I'm in the city, I like to play recordings of falling rain or birds singing in the background to relax my mind and body. If we can't go into the wilderness physically, our minds can trick our bodies into thinking we're there, and we can experience some benefits without leaving our armchairs!

EXERCISE

Reflect on your everyday actions and the built environments you live and work in. In what ways are you separated from the rest of creation in daily life? What small changes could you make to help yourself be more in sync?

Many of us associate synchronicity with specific experiences of feeling like the stars aligned and somehow magically things came together and seemed just right. Such moments are beautiful. I encourage you to imagine your entire life as a never-ending series of such moments. Think about synchronicity as a lifestyle, a way of being. If that sounds crazy, can you imagine what it is like to be a non-human? Do you think a plant's stem complains of pain during a big growth spurt, or that its leaves refuse to photosynthesise because they're experiencing self-hatred and can't allow in any nourishment? That's hard to imagine within the nature of a plant. The sad thing is, not only are we humans creating stress for ourselves and the rest of creation by being out of sync, we also tend to project fear and blame onto other beings and misread what's happening, placing ourselves in the role of victim instead of seeing a fuller picture of our impact on shared environments.

When walking the medicine wheel in everyday life, where we place our focus makes a huge difference to our lived experience. The lower world, the invisible, mysterious and intuited world of Mother Earth, is a metaphor for our state of being. And from our state of being emerges our actions in the physical, visible world of Father Sky. By focusing on embodying our values, we tend to feel more solid, like the trunk or roots of a tree. When focusing on specific actions and situations we tend to feel more like a leaf in a breeze. There is a concept from Native American cultures called the 'Red Road' that helps guide us. An image illustrating it[1] shows people on the Red Road focusing much more on the lower than the upper world, with about 80 per cent of their energy on living their values and cultivating intentional states of being and only 20 per cent on physical actions. This guideline can help with both daily decision-making, as well as long-term visioning and openness to the Unknown.

Consider your experience when someone gives you their full attention versus when they're multitasking, or how food tastes, feels and digests when you carefully cook and serve it or when you mindlessly consume takeaway in front of a screen. If I see trash on the beach and feel grumpy with judgemental thoughts about careless people, I'm not the right person to pick that rubbish up, because doing so would pile on more trash spiritually, emotionally and mentally! My work is then processing some rubbish inside myself so I can embody my core values and having faith that another person in a better state of being will pick up that piece of trash instead of me.

Unprocessed emotions, traumas and stories or beliefs are often our biggest blocks to being in synchronicity. Cree people teach seven ways of releasing negative emotions: crying, yelling, talking, sweating, singing, dancing and praying.[2] We also need regular grounding and clearing practices to return to, retrain and retain our desired states of being. Meditation and journeying are invaluable clearing practices, opportunities to hear inner voices, practise compassion, connect with intuition and deep self-honesty and let go, creating space for a bit more synchronicity. Let's consider the impact of our state of being on our non-human relatives in the exercise below.

EXERCISE

Watch the video of animal communicator Anna Breytenbach explaining why great white sharks get close to shore and how to safely coexist with them.[3] What do you think about the impact of your state of mind or energy on other beings? What about the perspective that our non-human kin are holding us in compassion?

Empathy

WEEK BEGINNING: _____

SEASON: _____

In week 19 we empathised with our non-human relatives. Empathy may include being sensitive to another's feelings, imagining or understanding another's experience, or even vicariously experiencing another's reality. Empathy can thus be experienced across the medicine wheel – mentally (understanding), physically (vicarious), emotionally (sensitive) and/or spiritually (imagining).

EXERCISE

Take a moment to reflect on how you tend to experience empathy.

Empathy can be a difficult gift to unpack. Many of us have had our gift developed through being intimate with people exhibiting narcissistic and bullying or bipolar personalities. This seems to be a common ordeal for empaths to navigate – how to honour and protect ourselves around people who do not have the capacity to see and respect our sensitivities. We learn our biggest spiritual lessons through ordeals. And much of learning in invisible, felt and intuited spaces involves seeing ourselves through the reflection another provides. What better way to see the depth of our gift of empathy more clearly than to be face to face with someone very much lacking it?

In Western culture if a child is a talented runner, chances are they will be noticed. And if they want to develop that gift, they will likely find support and start training for increasingly challenging races. Each big race is an ordeal, and each push to be a little bit faster or go a little farther may be experienced as a death and leap of faith into the Unknown. But in Western culture if you are a gifted empath as a child you may seem emotionally volatile and dysregulated, be put down for being 'overly sensitive' or withdraw into an isolated inner world and feel like you are performing in the outer world. In cultures where empathy is more understood and valued, children with empathic gifts are more likely to be noticed. This means that Elders can put these children through training and ordeals to develop their gift of empathy through a gentler process than we are used to in Western culture, similar to the runner.

One of the challenges of limited (or negative) support when developing a gift of empathy as a child is forming a clear understanding of self and other, and with that knowledge learning to set healthy boundaries. A lot of empathic children take on the emotions and unintegrated aspects of family members as part of their own identity. Let me give an example. A child who is highly sensitive has a hard time being with the intensity of stress in their household. They retreat to an isolated inner world to cope and spend a lot of time in their imagination. The child's retreating triggers an overwhelmed parent, who yells at the child for being selfish and lazy. If the child does need to do more around the house, that isn't a useful (or adult) way to tell them. The child feels ashamed and internalises the belief 'I am selfish and lazy.' With a skewed understanding of their own sense of self and worth, the child starts engaging in self-destructive behaviours and cultivates relationships with people who blame and punish them. The child won't heal that shame until they realise their parents' words were untrue, create accountability for self and others and learn to value and protect their self-worth.

We can have deep love for ourselves and others while still holding each person accountable for hurtful behaviours. Having compassion for wounds and limitations isn't the same as making excuses and minimising what's happening. The truth is often a paradox – the adult may have done their best to be a loving parent, *and* in a state of overwhelm took out frustration on the child that was deeply damaging to the child's emerging identity. Both of those can be true at once. Our Western minds are taught to label people (good parent, bad parent) and see that as a fixed identity. It's black and white thinking, and it's damaging. The more space we make for complexity and nuance, the more space there is for healing and simply being human.

EXERCISE

Set an intention over the next few days to notice where your mind is labelling yourself or others, and you are engaging in black and white thinking. What are the underlying beliefs or judgements creating those poor thought habits?

Poor thought habits can be changed, just like any other changes in our lives, by first practising acceptance. That's often 90 per cent of the work, to be able to admit to ourselves and see clearly what is happening, and our role in a painful relational dynamic. If we continue with the example above, most likely the healing journey for that empathic child will be complicated. They will realise that certain things aren't their responsibility, and that some people feel emotionally, mentally and spiritually dangerous to be with. They may realise they were doing 80 per cent of the emotional labour with a partner, which is draining and unsustainable. After a while, they may try being intimate with another partner, and through an iterative process learn to let go of identifying as selfish and lazy and start to become aware of and appreciate their sensitivities. Eventually they may find another partner similarly as sensitive. They will need to communicate carefully, teach each other how to treat each other, navigate their triggers and help each other heal.

That's an example of a journey of an empath who went deep into an isolated inner world as a child. Other empathic children may act out the overwhelming emotions they are experiencing and be put on drugs to numb their feelings and calm their behaviours, rather than the family realising their impact on the child. Being an empathic child is often like being an invisible canary in a coal mine – because in a coal mine, when the canary is sick, people know that means the environment is toxic.

Deep inside of us there is an impulse to heal and feel whole. We may not realise it consciously, but we tend to feel a calling of a journey towards healing and wholeness. And when we do learn who we are and come to terms with our empathy, it is an incredibly enriching gift. We have the opportunity to experience life very deeply and fully. We see things other people don't see and we learn so much, gaining wisdom beyond our years.

We also learn how we are impacted by different environments (physical, social or emotional and so on) and find ways to take better care of ourselves. This might mean avoiding certain places that stress us out like busy shopping malls or wearing earplugs if we have to go there. It may mean moving to the country because the pace of the city feels overwhelming, or ending a friendship when the other is blaming us for something. Empaths often have the foresight to notice danger before others. When a new boss starts and people are singing their praises about how nice they are, an empath feels cognitive dissonance in their presence and knows something isn't right. When the boss is later found to have been involved in illegal activity, the empath isn't surprised. If only more people trusted their instincts!

EXERCISE

Do you identify as sensitive and/or empathic? What do you like about that gift? What do you struggle with? How could you honour your gift a bit more?

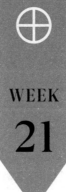

Boundaries

WEEK BEGINNING: _____

SEASON: _____

Boundaries are about our integrity, our wholeness. They are dependent on context or environment, identity and self-awareness of our needs and values and relate to all areas of the medicine wheel: mental, emotional, physical and spiritual. It's easiest to understand physical integrity, though concepts like consent and personal space differ by individual and culture. Spiritual integrity means upholding our faith, beliefs, rituals and ceremonial practices. Emotional integrity requires intimate self-knowledge and a full expression of our feelings. Mental boundaries tend to be the hardest to maintain, and we often ignore them because we are used to having busy minds. But as discussed in week 20, we can change poor thought habits.

Boundaries allow us to feel safe and secure enough to move through life with a heart that is appropriately open and protected, depending on the situation we're in. Integrity isn't about showing your heart to everybody and being vulnerable all the time; it's about knowing yourself and your context so well that you are protective, aware and alert when you're around vampires or crocodiles, and relaxed and at ease otherwise when it is safe to be. I see a lot of confusion around boundaries and a lot of misguided effort to 'set' them, resulting in drama, mind games and power plays. We can't bypass our healing through intellectually understanding something; we need to have lived experiences for the knowledge to be grounded and fully integrated in our lives across the whole medicine wheel.

For example, you might feel aversion about going on a blind date. You may have heard horror stories from friends and decided it's not for you. And life may not present you with any opportunities, so that may be an easy mental boundary to maintain. But if two friends separately say they want to set you up on a blind date with someone, and then you have a dream about being on a date with someone you don't recognise, you may be denying yourself a learning and healing opportunity by maintaining the mental boundary.

When we get repeated Indigenous science data like this and ignore it, we invite trouble and loss. Instead, we can choose to take the opportunities life presents to free ourselves from carrying pain by experiencing it fully, allowing ourselves to heal and embodying the medicine or learnings.

Better boundaries emerge through our healing process as we come into more integrity. And as we gain trust in our healing journey and build confidence in our discernment abilities, we realise when we feel called to go through an ordeal and which battles are not ours. So much of being in integrity is getting our 'yeses' and 'noes' into alignment with our core values and listening to Indigenous science data in daily life.

When we are whole, or in integrity, we are boundaried. Upholding our boundaries in such a state arises involuntarily and naturally. If someone stomps on my foot, I say 'Ow!' or 'Hey!' without thinking, and if someone behaves disrespectfully, my voice will rise in volume or my tone will become a bit harsher. We want boundaries that aren't so rigid when they're crossed we blow up like volcanoes, nor so loose that we are pushovers putting others' needs ahead of ours, nor so flimsy that we allow ourselves to be neglected or abused. When we freeze, or feel shame, guilt or fear of reprisal when our boundaries are tested or we aren't aware until later that our boundaries have been crossed, we have some work to do.

The first thing to consider is context or environment. We may (inadvertently) be putting ourselves into dangerous situations, either because we don't know better or are taking a risk that could be better mitigated. Some environments are dangerous by their nature; for example, if I knew as a young woman getting drunk at a party where I didn't know anybody was likely putting myself into a dangerous situation. It doesn't mean that if someone crosses our boundaries that it's our fault – people are still responsible for their own behaviour – but it does mean we didn't do a great job protecting ourselves from that environment or within it once we were there. If I were mitigating that party risk, I would likely have had friends with me and we'd be watching out for each other, counting drinks, have a designated driver and leave together.

The second thing to consider is identity, and the most common wound is low self-worth. We may feel guilty or ashamed to stand up for ourselves, scared that the other person will punish us or righteously angry that we 'shouldn't' have to deal with something because it's 'wrong'. Righteous anger helps clarify our values, but it's not good at setting secure boundaries because it's usually based in judgement. We can hold the moral value that abuse is wrong, while still accepting that abuse happens and having compassion for all involved. It also helps to have faith that if something comes up (especially more than once), there's something in it for us.

When we ignore, deny and/or judge thoughts, feelings and experiences, we are telling parts of our self that they're not worthy of time and attention, placing those aspects of our being into shame and fear. If you are scared of being punished, you may need to show yourself that you are worthy of fighting for, and that if someone is abusive you are willing to confront that person and/or end a relationship if needed. And if you want inspiration, cats are great teachers for guilt-free upholding of their boundaries and shamelessly seeking fulfilment of their needs!

Third, consider your needs and core values. It could be that you are still learning some of your needs. When we are abused and/or neglected as children, it takes time as adults to unpack it, grieve our losses and learn how to create new and healthier experiences for ourselves. Sometimes we feel numb to danger due to negative traumatic experiences that pushed our nervous systems into functioning at a level of hyper alertness. Practices like body relaxation, grounding or earthing and spending time in wilderness help calm our nervous systems. But if you're still intimate with someone who's neglecting and/or abusing you, those practices will only help you build resilience, not heal. It's important to discern the difference, and not judge yourself about where you're at. If you feel unsafe around someone or in a certain space, it doesn't need to logically 'make sense'. Let go of the need to explain yourself to anyone, including your own mind. Emotions follow their own logic, and the mind may need to sit in the Unknown for a while as you reflect on which feelings are based on a wound you need to work through, and which are based on insight or intuition that it would be wise to trust and honour.

EXERCISE

What does integrity mean to you (spiritually, emotionally, physically and mentally)? Where do you feel strongly in integrity? Take time to imagine and experience it.

Now reflect on where your boundaries are being tested and/or you feel out of integrity. Considering context or environment, identity and awareness of your needs and values, reflect on why and what you could do to heal. What are you avoiding or resisting?

Addiction

WEEK BEGINNING: _____

SEASON: _____

Trauma and addiction are interrelated, and Dr Gabor Maté, a Western medical doctor specialising in addiction and trauma treatment, says freezing (as in the survival strategies of fight, flight, freeze or fawn) is meant to be a temporary state that we heal from to regain integrity and peace when the survival threat has gone.[1] But what if the threat doesn't go away? For example, as a child you may spend years living with an abusive parent, and most of us are still living with the daily impacts of colonisation. Growing up with ongoing threats is tough, and Maté reminds us that developmentally, babies and children are narcissistic (self-oriented). When we are forming a sense of self and feel rejected, unsafe and unwanted, we naturally (and narcissistically) think *we're* the problem, that we're 'not good enough'. This makes the rejection existential, integrating shame into our very identity. This shamed self can become normalised and persist intergenerationally in families, or even cultures.

Since addictions develop when parts of ourselves have felt unsafe and unwanted, to heal we might need to sit with inner spaces that are a bit ugly, filled with resentment and mistrust. It takes effort to rebuild a relationship with a part of ourselves that was rejected. For example, if you were shamed for being lazy, as your own parent, you can live so that resting and going slowly is something you value. In that way, you teach yourself the positive side of being lazy, accept and move through hard feelings and thoughts you took on as a child, and heal through a positive alternate experience.

One way we tend to process immense trauma and pain is to focus on things that feel better, which is understandable, because to be healthy we do need to experience some pleasure. But we often overindulge to our detriment and get caught in a cycle of addiction. Addictions can include all areas of the medicine wheel. For example, we may become mentally addicted to negative or positive thought patterns – such as 'I am a loser' or 'I am successful', denying alternate feedback and missing learning opportunities. We may become emotionally addicted to certain experiences such as novelty or intensity and miss out on the joys of sustaining and deepening relationships and enjoying subtler pleasures. Spiritually, we may become addicted to powerful altered states of consciousness, such through using psychedelics, at the expense of subtler, yet equally profound experiences such as star gazing or communing with a bird in a garden. And physically, many of us are familiar with addictions to food, alcohol, sugar, caffeine, cigarettes, and other substances that momentarily feel good but overall leave us feeling unsated so that we keep looking for more. Addiction is the lived experience of never enough – the nature of Wetiko.

But rejection, even existential rejection, like any feeling or experience, can be approached with openness, curiosity and even playfulness. We can reject with gentle words and tone, allow saving face if culturally important, and try 'not to take it personally' by seeking honest feedback when in doubt. We can also avoid rejection in ways that tend to be cowardly, such as 'ghosting' someone or lying (through omission or otherwise) when someone we care about would be open to honest feedback. It's tough to navigate rejection, and it helps to give ourselves and others grace. Three strategies that can help are practising acceptance without expectation, allowing change to emerge over time; choosing any survival strategy to avoid freezing to break old patterns; and creating safe space for vulnerability and honesty.

EXERCISE

Reflect on an area of your life where you feel not good enough and/or where you experience an addictive behaviour. Is there an underlying belief about yourself that you can challenge through changing your lived experience to facilitate healing? How are you practising the three strategies for navigating rejection?

The core of these wounds are experiences of existential rejection, and most of us carry such wounds from when we and/or our ancestors were forcibly moved off traditional lands, forced to adopt unfamiliar cultural practices and forms of spiritual worship, forced to live in homes, wear clothes and eat foods that were unfamiliar and were otherwise abused and/or enslaved. Such traumas teach us to be ashamed of what our ancestors taught us about how to live, where to live and what to honour. We become disempowered, ungrounded, disoriented, and struggle to maintain healthy, whole identities and cultures. We feel overpowered and lied to, and we often feel deep in our bones that something is wrong. We wonder if we're crazy, if something is wrong with us, and we feel abandoned and angry with our families and society. For many of us, we and/or our ancestors both experienced this rejection, as well as perpetrated it. Sifting through those complexities takes time. It is decolonisation work that exposes many layers of trauma and addiction (personal, familial, communal, cultural and ancestral).

One way to address these layers is through ancestral healing.[2] Consider the exercise on the next page about remembering our identity and ancestry.

EXERCISE

Fill in the blanks:

I am _____. I was born on _____ land where the _____ people are traditional
      [name(s)]   [ceded/unceded*]   [culture(s)]

custodians. I was born in_____in/on a_____. I feel most at home in____
                [season]   [climactic zone** biome***]   [season]

on _____. The language I feel most natural speaking is _____and I am most
   [climactic zone]   [language]

fluent in _____. I was raised _____, and I practise _____. My_____ heritage
          [language]   [spirituality]   [spirituality]   [patrilineal]

is/are_____, and my matrilineal is/are _____. My partner's heritage includes
        [culture(s)]   [culture(s)]

_____. I feel a connection with _____, _____. My personal, family, clan and/or
  [culture(s)]   [culture(s)] [place(s)]

nation totems† and moiety†† are_____. I now live and work on ancestral land
                                [totems, moiety]

of the _____ people. It is a_____. Important landforms include_____,
       [culture(s)]   [climactic zone biome]   [landforms]

and the water I drink comes from _____. Winds predominantly flow _____.
                                 [water source(s)]   [direction]

My electrical power comes from _____. The main spirituality here is _____.
                               [power source(s)]   [spirituality]

I feel most centred and at peace _____.
                                 [when/where/with whom]

How did it feel to fill this out? What surprised
you? What do/did you not know?

....

....

....

....

....

....

* Was there a fair treaty ceding traditional lands to another people?
** For example, tropical, alpine, temperate and so on.
*** For example, savanna, forest, tundra, mountainous and so on.
† Non-human being/s with whom you have a sacred responsibility of protection and care taking.
†† Kinship structure of descent and social responsibilities.

Desire and need

WEEK BEGINNING: _____

SEASON: _____

W eek 22's closing exercise is a reminder to me that despite our collective efforts to pollute, desecrate and otherwise disrespect the planet, our non-human kin and each other, Mother Earth still supports us to survive. Most of us humans still have air to breathe, water to drink, food to eat, shelter and fire (from power stations or actual fires) to keep us warm, and social lives and cultural stories to keep up our spirits.

When we have inherited or internalised trauma, shame and resentment, or experienced abuse and neglect, it can be hard to maintain faith that life always provides what we need. There is an epidemic of deficit-based thinking on the planet. Wetiko has become embedded into our social structures and altered our collective worldview so that we sustain oppressive hierarchies and create scarcity for ourselves and our non-human kin. It might seem audacious in the face of this to have faith that we always receive what we need. I'll tell you some of my journey and how this helped me.

Growing up I had shelter, but it wasn't safe; I had food, but it didn't nourish me (due to undiagnosed digestive disease); I had air, but it was filled with chemicals as I wasn't allowed to open any windows; I had water, but it was so chlorinated I broke out in rashes; I had fire, but it was generated mainly from coal (not the cleanest); and I had cultural stories that both sustained me and felt destructive, with an isolated social life revolving around my family. This was not the most nourishing childhood, but it wasn't the least nourishing either. I survived with limited supports.

Some of my struggles have taken decades of hard work to reconcile. As an adult, there are many things we can do to heal wounds but there are some things we can only grieve and move on from. For example, I had a strong desire to do gymnastics as a child. But my brother wanted to play soccer, and my parents said it was easier for them that we did the same thing. I didn't like soccer, but I did my best for a few seasons. As a teenager I found yoga, which felt related to gymnastics, and dove deeply into that. I looked for adult gymnastics classes but my body wasn't up for tumbles and jumps like a child's, so instead I grieved it as a missed experience.

When we don't grieve such losses, we carry resentment and project unfulfilled childhood desires onto our children instead of seeing and supporting their desires, as well as helping them process losses of their own. I have found that through processing losses, not only am I able to support others through their struggles but that my tough experiences taught me the difference between need and desire. This has led me today to focusing my life on supporting my basic needs, and taught me when to let go of a desire and grieve.

EXERCISE

Reflect on what you need to survive: spiritually, mentally, emotionally and physically. Consider doing the medicine wheel exercise from week 2, where you make note of your needs in each area and the heart centre (in consideration of your core values). How well do you prioritise your needs? How much does your life revolve around them?

Deficit and greed go hand in hand. Societies with the biggest differences in material resources between 'rich' and 'poor' are filled with deficit thinking and greedy behaviour. Many people admire philanthropists like Bill Gates for 'giving away' money, but to put yourself in the position of hoarding so many physical resources that you have to work to give them away (and even then control how that happens) is, in Indigenous science, the path of a greedy individualist with a saviour complex. Why else would someone hoard so much more than they need when everything they consume out of greed denies others the opportunity to simply be?

Torres Islander scientist Nonie Sharp sees social relationships as based in mateship or in-mateship.[1] In-mateship creates feelings of worthlessness, self-hatred and denial because the very presence of superiority creates shame, and a fear of shame causes people to oscillate between seeking revenge and prestige, resulting in psychic bullying, social violence and denying reciprocity. If you judge someone as an in-mate, you control and define social and existential boundaries. When there is lack or denial of reciprocity in a relationship, we tend to feel resentfully stifled and unseen because the other person isn't holding us in wholeness, while the person lost in judgement and trying to control things tends to experience lack, denial, shame and ungroundedness because they are cut off from experiencing wholeness and reciprocity.

We cannot force anyone into reciprocity; we can only maintain healthy boundaries and have compassion for those who do not feel whole and behave through force, control and other forms of desecration and destruction. What people lost in judgement and control need (whether they are playing either role in the in-mateship relationship described above) is to re-member their Indigenous roots and open their hearts and minds to altered states of consciousness to cultivate different thinking habits and ways of being. When we realise a relationship isn't meeting our basic needs, we can either try to work on it together with the other, change it through boundary setting or end it altogether.

Our most basic needs are intimately intertwined with the needs of the Earth and our non-human kin. In Indigenous science, the sacred reciprocity of an 'Honourable Harvest' applies to all interactions and exchanges between humans and the Earth. A definition from Potawatomi scientist

Dr Robin Wall Kimmerer is: 'Ask permission of the ones whose lives you seek. Abide by the answer. Never take the first. Never take the last. Harvest in a way that minimizes harm. Take only what you need . . . Use everything that you take . . . Share it, as the Earth has shared with you.'[2]

You may be wondering how you can, or already are, reciprocating the gifts the Earth gives you. We can do so in many ways, including:

⊙ expressing gratitude
⊙ doing ceremony and sacred ritual
⊙ caring for the Earth, including caring for human and non-human kin
⊙ creating art and music honouring the Earth
⊙ engaging in acts of creative resistance against social structures that go against our values, including how we spend our money and time.

EXERCISE

Reflect on the Honourable Harvest, 'a covenant of reciprocity between humans and the land'. Reflect on how well you embody this in your daily life, and where you struggle. How do you reciprocate the gifts the Earth gives you? What would life be like if the Honourable Harvest was socially supported and upheld?

Trickster

WEEK BEGINNING: _____

SEASON: _____

Creation stories around the world teach that trickster was our creator, such as the raven[1] among several cultures in the northern US and Canada, the serpent tricking Eve in the Bible, Loki in Norse mythology, coyote among numerous Native American cultures and the spider Anansi among many African and Caribbean cultures. Trickster[2] is an archetypal earthly figure whose gifts include shapeshifting, cleverness, foolishness, greediness, sneakiness and a lack of a moral compass. They frequently act on whims and enjoy boundary pushing, as well as creating chaos and confusion.

Trickiness is a part of our nature. Sometimes we purposely trick ourselves as a form of self-care, like when we are in pain and think about our 'happy place' to feel better. We often play tricks with children with the intention of protecting them and playing pretend, such as telling them that Grandpa will be okay when we don't know if that's true when he's rushed to the hospital with a heart attack, or that a magical tooth fairy left them a dollar. But trickster has a dark side, like everything on Earth, and there are downright scary ways we trick ourselves and others, like denying we have a drinking problem, getting wasted and then recklessly driving ourselves home.

When we engage in rigid, binary, black and white thinking with bright line rules of right and wrong without nuance, we deny (and therefore feed) trickster aspects of our being. That's because trickster energy exists in defiance of an established order; they are agents of chaos. This is why so many communities proudly proclaiming they are values based are shocked when one of their leaders has a sex scandal emerge, or something similar. When suppressed and denied, trickster aspects of our being inevitably find a way to be expressed, usually through our most taboo thoughts, feelings and, ultimately, behaviours. It's as if life is forcing us to reconcile and make peace with our deepest fears and aversions, to make space for the complexity of being human. It's hard to continue believing, for example, that being gay is 'wrong' if your own daughter comes out, and even harder if you start to feel urges inside yourself.

When Trump was elected president of the US I saw many liberal-minded people quite upset, saying that their understanding of the society and systems of governance we were part of had been shaken to the core. But I felt like his victory was an honest reflection of the nation I had grown up in, and I hoped it would show that the emperor had no clothes, that so much of the story people believe about the US is based more on rhetoric than reality. The most recent US presidential election seems to have helped more people become aware that our current systems are unsustainable.

I am reminded of the Albert Einstein quote that you can't solve a problem with the same consciousness that created it, and I don't think that consciousness raising, despite well-meaning rhetoric, is the answer. I don't see consciousness as something we can 'raise' in each other as much as something we choose to alter on a path of healing and spiritual homecoming. As Anishinaabe Elder Isaac Murdoch said in relation to the coronavirus: 'The elders are reminding us to go back to the land. And so, for us, the land is the biggest healthcare system, and so we know that through the cultural practices of how we survived great sicknesses before, that the land is the answer.'[3]

In Indigenous science well-being is grounded in country, including trickster energy. A trickster hippopotamus hides underwater, and when a jackal dips its head for a drink it's stealthily snapped up. A trickster opossum freezes and plays dead when it sees a wolf, knowing the wolf prefers a fresh kill. But much of our modern human trickster energy is ungrounded and results in mind games. These days some politicians are tricking people into thinking (and believing) that the coronavirus doesn't exist, and some of those very politicians have then died of the coronavirus.[4]

Three keys to healthfully embodying our trickster aspect of being are to: (1) accept it with humility; (2) keep a sense of humour about it; and (3) purposely engage and play with it to honour it in our lives. The first one may seem obvious, but sometimes when we are tricked, even in small ways, it outrages us or otherwise hurts our individual sense of identity so that we miss opportunities to accept it. Awareness of our binary thoughts or beliefs, especially related to our sense of identity, is empowering and limits our playing trickster without meaning to. Let's say someone believes only 'good' people go to heaven, and so they work to be 'a good person' who 'never disrespects anyone'. When that person is told they have disrespected someone they likely block themselves from accepting it, because being respectful is a basis of their identity and their spiritual and social survival. This will intensify until their denial becomes harder to maintain.

The second key, keeping a sense of humour about trickster energy, prevents us from taking our moments of playing the fool too seriously. For example, a while ago I was taking a bag of Styrofoam peanuts out to the garbage bin when a gust of wind knocked the bag out of my hand, sending non-eco friendly peanuts down the street. I had a meeting to go to, which was why I foolishly didn't take a little extra time to knot the bag before going outside on a windy morning. Ultimately, I was late to the meeting from picking up peanuts, but when I arrived and told the story we all had a good laugh. Of course, some tricks we fall for are destructive and are harder to find humour in. After investing a lot of money in a sham, it takes time to forgive yourself and the person who tricked you, grieve and feel light-hearted enough to joke about it.

The third key of being intentionally tricky at times is often hardest for us. Ways to honour it include playing practical jokes, acting and playing pretend (from acting to writing fiction to doing visualisation-based meditations), playing devil's advocate and questioning norms and 'knowns', being spontaneous and acting on a whim, embracing some chaos, lying for a short time (for example, for a surprise party) and mindfully pushing boundaries and social norms (from a man trying on a skirt to being a full-on drag queen).

EXERCISE

What is your relationship with trickster? How do you feel when you realise you've been tricked? How do you feel about playing the fool and being the butt of a joke? How do you purposely play with and honour trickster energy?

WEEK

25

The elements

WEEK BEGINNING: _____

SEASON: _____

The most common elements of a medicine wheel are earth, air, fire and water, with the heart centre linked to the ethereal. Our lives are made up of these elements: our bodies are filled with watery blood, our lungs with life-sustaining air, our bones with earthy minerals and our vitality is defined by our fiery animating spirits.

It is called a 'medicine wheel' because it offers medicine to us through wisdom and guidance on a life journey. Every culture has a medicine wheel, whether we are aware of it or not, each with its own worldview filled with vital symbols, messages and metaphors linked to the land. Some medicine wheels are not in four parts and use different elements, such as the traditional Chinese medicine wheel that is divided into five equal parts, representing fire, water, wood, metal and earth.[1] If you do not already know your medicine wheel, let's divine it now. If you already know your wheel, skip the following exercise and read on.

EXERCISE

Set an intention to divine your medicine wheel. Smudge, pray, leave an offering at your ancestral altar or otherwise open sacred space and ground and centre yourself.

Gather plain paper and coloured drawing tools. Draw a circle. (You may wish to trace a bowl.) Ask yourself intuitively how your medicine wheel is divided, then create segments. Using your non-dominant hand, intuitively pick up a drawing tool and colour in a segment. Ask yourself which element is associated with it. Do that for the remaining segments. Ask yourself if there is a colour to put around the boundary of your wheel, the area outside the wheel and/or at the centre.

Now intuitively ask yourself what else you may know about the wheel. You may get insight about plants, animals, seasons and cycles and so on linked with the segments of your wheel. When you feel complete, honour your wheel by placing it somewhere you will see it.

Your medicine wheel is a metaphorical map for your life, culture and state of being. Consider how you may integrate honouring the elements of your medicine wheel into your daily life. For example, you may set an intention to thank and bless the water when you wash your face or take a shower, or you may say a prayer for the air when you smudge your space. You may bless each element when you say your daily prayers. The elements represent fundamental life energies, and it is powerful to intentionally honour them.

In general, Indigenous science ceremonies and rituals tend to intentionally honour all the elements of a medicine wheel. For example, when I am doing a smudging ceremony, I honour the earth through the offering of the plant that will be smudged, the fire by using its spark to light the plant, the air through the smoke that cleanses the space and the water by spraying essential oil diluted in water into the space to clear the lingering smoke and close the ceremony.

Some ceremonies and rituals honour specific elements. For example, the summer solstice for me is about honouring the sun, the sacred masculine, a big ball of fire. For a few years, my husband has led our summer solstice fire ceremony with a Celtic cultural practice from Galicia of making queimada: putting clear brandy, fruit, sugar (and sometimes coffee beans) into a ceramic bowl, then lighting a spoonful of the mixture while saying prayers of thanksgiving and protection, and continually keeping the fire going by using the spoon to lift and pour bits of fiery liquid prayers back into the bowl.[2] When the fire goes out, we gift some of the drink to Mother Earth, leave some as an offering on our ancestral altars and drink some ourselves. This is not the only ceremony we do on the solstice, but it is a significant one to honour the element of fire at that time of year.

Some people feel called to honour an element with its own altar. For example, I have seen a water altar with bottles of water from different places, along with seashells, river rocks, a mermaid statue and other watery symbols. We can also honour the elements at important life ceremonies. As I write this, I am preparing for childbirth and have been reflecting about how we will ceremonially honour the elements at the birth. For example, I may wipe a feather across the newborn's body and recite blessings that loved ones have shared, give birth in a tub to honour water, rub some clay from the garden on the baby's feet to honour the earth and connect with this land and light a candle on my ancestral altar to honour fire and acknowledge an ancestor being born. So much of honouring is about intention and awareness, so you may have some traditions where you can intentionally honour the elements without changing any rituals. For example, a christening may honour water by pouring it on the baby's head, air through spoken prayers for the baby, earth by placing oil on the baby's body and fire by lighting a candle for the baby's spirit.

If you look around there are altars everywhere, and it can be fun and fulfilling to tend them with more intention. For example, many of us honour specific aspects of the earth, such as keeping potted plants in our homes or displaying crystals, but we don't tend to think about it that way. Many of us have altars for specific aspects of fire, such as honouring the spirit of the Virgin Mary or Lord Ganesh with statues and candles, or the spirit of family with photos and mementos on our mantle. The storage space for your dishes could be seen as an altar to the earth, fire and craftsmanship that created them, even if you don't know where they are from. And showers, sinks and bathtubs may be seen as altars honouring water. If you know where your water comes from you can thank local rain clouds, rivers and/or reservoirs when you wash, as well as pipes carrying the water to you, re-membering the water in a grounded way.

EXERCISE

Set an intention to pay attention to how you may more intentionally honour the elements in your home and garden and daily practices, and on special occasions. Now walk around your space looking for altars. What are you honouring in your space? Is there anything you'd like to honour that you aren't? Is there anything you're honouring that doesn't feel right?

Keep in mind that in some ways we all honour systems like capitalism that we are collectively part of, so be gentle with yourself. You may wish to write down and/or share your insights and intentions with a support person to help you integrate them into your life by creating accountability.

WEEK

26

Altar work

WEEK BEGINNING: _____

SEASON: _____

An altar practice is a beautiful way to honour different beings and energies, deepen your relationships with their spirit and receive powerful guidance and insight. Week 25 was closed by reflecting on what you are honouring with home altars, and what you would like to intentionally honour. An altar can be created to honour nearly anything, and the amount of time and effort you put into tending and connecting with it is personal to you (though I do suggest at a minimum keeping them clean). In weeks 6 and 7 we began our altar journey with guidance on creating an ancestral altar and connecting with a tree to begin an outdoor altar practice. If you haven't continued to engage with those practices, I encourage you to revisit the chapters and see if you now have the drive to maintain an ancestral altar and/or outdoor altar.

If you divined your medicine wheel in week 25, or you already know it, a powerful practice that I have been doing for years is working with a medicine wheel altar. Most wheels have layers of metaphor and meaning in each segment, such as directionality (north, east, west and south); an element; a totem (usually plant or animal); a colour; and an aspect of life (spiritual, mental, emotional and physical). Through medicine wheel altar work we get a mirror of our journey around the wheel as well as a reflection of our state of being along the way.

For me, working with this altar at the start and end of my day has for many years been my most powerful tool for self-reflection. This has been especially valuable to me as I have not been blessed with wise Elders who know me intimately and can offer insights about my personal growth and blind spots. My medicine wheel altar practice has evolved over time as I gained clarity and insight. For example, I started with a cloth medicine wheel in the typical colours of Native Americans who were sharing knowledge with me (red, white, black and yellow). I put a salt lamp on the altar for a while until I realised that the bright light represented Grandfather Sun and needed to be outside the cloth, held in sacred tension with an object representing Grandmother Moon. I had a figurine of a joyful little girl on the altar until I healed childhood trauma and felt moved to bury it as a gift to Earth. Then I knew I was ready to embody that joy through my inner child instead of praying for it at the altar. A gold Star of David necklace from childhood was on the altar until I felt it was time to gift it to water and free myself from what felt like the greed of gold and the yoke of religion.

Over time I learned the colours of my wheel, created a new one and gifted my original cloth to fire. I start and end each day with prayers at my medicine wheel altar, and once a week I smudge and spray essential oil over it. I hope that gives you some insight into this kind of altar work.

EXERCISE

Using paper, canvas or cloth, create a two-dimensional medicine wheel the size of a large pizza that will be in your private space (maybe on a shelf, table or dresser). Cleanse the wheel with smudge or another tool. If you know how your wheel aligns with the four directions, use a compass to place the altar cloth so that the centre of the east direction of your cloth is facing due east. If you do not know the directions of your wheel, you can still use a compass to learn the directions in your space and intuitively choose which colour of your wheel feels right to face each direction.

Intuitively place power objects on and around the altar. I suggest starting simply with one or two objects in each direction, and a few around the outer edges of the wheel if that feels right. Perhaps you know that north represents the crow totem on your wheel so you place a crow feather there. Or maybe you picked up a rock on a recent walk and feel moved to place it on your wheel. Over time as you work with the wheel you will gain insight into why you placed objects where you did, and you will know through the clair senses, signs, visions, dreams and other Indigenous science data when to remove objects and how to let them go.

Set an intention to check in with yourself and your journey through your reflection in the wheel. It's okay to spend time with it daily, weekly or randomly. Trust the process. And when you get insight to do something with the wheel, follow through. It is a way to show up for yourself and avoid bringing destruction into your world.

We often hear the phrase about our bodies being temples, and one way to honour that is through body altar work. It may be as mundane as intentionally honouring different body parts as you soap in the shower or put on lotion. It may be doing the embodied medicine wheel practice from week 2, or it may be through wearing particular clothing or doing certain kinds of dance or movement. Let's reflect on this further.

EXERCISE

What does a body altar practice mean to you? Do what comes to you and see how it feels. Set an intention to repeat your body altar practice this week and notice how you feel when you do it (and if you don't).

In addition to our bodies being sacred, our homes are also sacred. Most spaces designated 'spiritual' such as temples, churches or even yoga classrooms are filled with prayers and power objects, candles and incense, beautiful artwork and peaceful chanting or music. Maybe that's not your idea of spiritual fulfilment, and you feel more joy listening to rock music on a leather sofa with a guitar hanging on the wall and the smell of beer and cigarettes in the air. What is sacred is very personal; there are no rules. I encourage you to think of your home as a sacred space embodying your values and worldview. Let's reflect further about what that means for you practically.

EXERCISE

Let's start by intentionally creating protective boundaries around your home. I suggest using rocks or crystals, but do what feels right to you if that doesn't resonate. Gather four objects to create protective energetic boundaries for your home. Ground and centre yourself, and smudge or otherwise cleanse the objects.

Go to each of the four directions (north, east, south and west) and place a rock in an innocuous place near the border of your home (such as inside a cupboard, on a windowsill or outside in the ground). I suggest placing them out of sight where others are unlikely to disturb them. As you place the object, allow intentions, prayers and blessings to flow through you. If it feels right, ask the spirit of each direction to keep your home and everyone who enters into it safe and secure.

Now, building on the reflection exercise from week 25, see if there are any changes that feel right to make in your home and garden altars. If so, make (or make plans) for the changes. When that feels complete, sit somewhere that feels like the centre of your home. Take a few deep breaths and relax. How do you feel in your temple?

Spiritual traps

WEEK BEGINNING: _____

SEASON: _____

T his week we're going to consider eight common spiritual traps we can fall into that take us away from Indigenous science, along with suggestions for freeing ourselves.

1. Spiritual vacations occur when we do something (like take a psychedelic),[1] or go somewhere (like a meditation retreat) that alters our consciousness, then find ourselves unable to integrate what we learned into daily life. Putting ourselves in a group environment allows some of us to access states of being we otherwise can't, just like some of us find that certain substances help us enter altered states of being.

Cultivating the self-discipline of a daily practice is a way out of this trap. Another is honest check-ins about our intentions, like: 'Am I reaching for this plant because I feel called to do sacred ceremony, or because I want to feel a certain way today?'

2. Sometimes we get addicted to intensity. This could look like anything from doing 30 ayahuasca ceremonies to being in relationships with lots of drama. Indigenous science is about balance, and we need to be able to deeply appreciate a range of experiences (emotionally, physically, mentally and spiritually).

The main way to break free is to detox by taking a break from the intensity, resetting boundaries and allowing ourselves to feel numb, grumpy and bored while we rebalance. With patience and persistence we regain the ability to enjoy more subtle states of being. For example, if you're used to hearing city traffic it'll take a while of being in the quiet of the country to be able to hear the wings of a butterfly when it flits by.

3. Spiritual bypass is a 'tendency to use spiritual ideas and practices to sidestep or avoid facing unresolved emotional issues, psychological wounds, and unfinished developmental tasks'.[2] Someone may believe that they must remain in an abusive relationship because of karma, or someone might be getting feedback they're behaving bossily and being controlling and excuse it as being a leader with high standards.

The first step out is being open to realising that we have been denying or suppressing something. Sometimes it takes multiple experiences, or wise counsel from someone we trust. The next step is facing the denial and seeking support to accept ourselves more fully.

4. Another trap is black and white thinking. In Indigenous science, 'Both dark and light are necessary for life.'[3] Unlike New Age 'go to the light' thinking, Indigenous scientists see darkness as the purest form of light because it contains all colours, whereas white reflects and rejects.[4] When we find ourselves existentially rejecting or judging (for example, 'cancel culture'), being 'objective' (for example, imposing our view onto others) and/or labelling (for example, calling someone a 'bad' person), we are engaged in black and white thinking.

To heal we must make space for grey areas, and find the humility to carry a little doubt even when we feel confident. Noticing our and others' existential crises (when we are highly triggered), we can then unpack why we and/or others feel so unsafe and shift beliefs.

5. Guru worship involves giving our power away to a being who 'knows better' on an existential level. When we place someone on a pedestal, we devalue ourselves. What we honour with our time is what we worship, and a guru may be non-human such as marijuana, mushrooms, alcohol or another being we give high status in our lives. Guru worship is the basis of most cults.

The main way to escape (as a giver or receiver) is to become aware of feeling devalued or pedestalled. And if you are using a substance with the intention of doing ceremony, I suggest stopping regularly to see if you experience any addictive urges, reflect on your relationship with the substance and work to purify it. For example, I know someone who stopped doing Native American tobacco pipe ceremonies the moment he realised he had picked it up to smoke without the intention of praying.

6. Spiritual ambition is tricky, because ambition is often rewarded in other areas of life. The saying that when the student is ready the teacher appears is wise. With each spiritual teaching comes responsibility. For example, if

you do a pipe ceremony, you enter into a sacred relationship with tobacco. If you then smoke a cigarette at a party, it not only won't be fun, but you may even become unwell for desecrating the plant.

I suggest reflecting on where your desires for new learnings are coming from, and taking a small step to see what feedback you get through Indigenous science data. For example, if you wish to carry your own medicine drum, you might start by placing a power object representing this desire on your ancestral altar and praying for guidance and support on that path. Then patiently see whether a step towards a drum emerges for you.

7. Spiritual businesses are another tricky aspect of modern life. What is spiritually wise (for example, telling a student they are not ready for a ceremony) may be very unwise in the business world. And sacred reciprocity isn't based on a transactional economy.

I suggest not making a spiritual business your sole survival strategy financially so it's easier to maintain integrity. It also helps to be willing to fail while doing what's right.

8. Cultural appropriation is using 'objects or elements of a non-dominant culture in a way that doesn't respect their original meaning, give credit to their source, or reinforces stereotypes or contributes to oppression practices'.[5] There's some nuance here, but it's important to consider when knowledge sharing with other cultures.

Try to be humbly honest with yourself about your intentions when learning and using other cultural knowledge, how you may be benefiting (socially, financially, politically and so on), how you are honouring the source of the knowledge and whether you are the right person to be further sharing other cultures' knowledge. It is valuable to be an ally, but keep in mind that allies do not lead unless they are asked.

EXERCISE

Reflect on the eight spiritual traps discussed this week. Which ones have you experienced? Which ones have you witnessed others go through? What helped you and those you know escape and avoid these traps?

Power

WEEK BEGINNING: _____

SEASON: _____

et's open this week with a quote:

When you know who you are; when your mission is clear and you burn with the inner fire of unbreakable will; no cold can touch your heart, no deluge can dampen your purpose. You know that you are alive. — attributed to Chief Seattle

In week 5 we discussed that power is based on our connection with the Earth and faith in an unseen, interconnected sacredness in the world. Let's now reflect on power in all areas of the medicine wheel. Power in the heart centre includes our identity, culture(s) and core values (week 3) that we carry and embody. Mental power includes clarity of discernment (week 15) and problem-solving skills as well as Wetiko (week 9) and trickster (week 24). Spiritual power includes our cosmology (week 10), creation story and ancestry (week 6), as well as shadow (week 14) aspects we haven't yet integrated. Physical power includes economic and material power, as well as grounding in our physical environment (week 4). And emotional power includes social status and privileges, lived experiences, traumas (week 11) and triggers, and relational dynamics with humans and non-humans.

Our personal power is thus a combination of many complex energies, and as Sioux[1] scientist Dr Vine Deloria Jr says: 'Power and place produce personality.'[2] Individuality is both an authentic expression in a moment as well as a relational recognition of an innate interconnectedness of being. The Lakota people honour this wisdom by ending all of their prayers and ceremonies with the phrase '*Aho Mitakuye Oyasin*', which translates as 'All my relations.'[3]

When we are able to hold our identity as both paradoxically timeless in Spirit and time bound as an embodied individual life, we experience a sense of wholeness and centeredness. If we lose touch with this, we identify with our wounds and often feel like victims even when we behave like offenders. When we are unable to fully feel and be alive with parts of our selves lost in shadow and existential judgement, we become 'living zombies . . . capable of committing great violence'[4] on ourselves and others. Indigenous science suggests that those of us who are involved in such violent behaviours, whether as victims, offenders or other impacted parties, carry some shame in our identities.[5] This shame, often called 'sin', is integrated into our self-beliefs, creating lived experiences of our perceived lack of worth and tragically reinforcing our existing wounds. This infinite loop of pain is often called the Cycle of Violence.[6]

Violent behaviour may be seen as 'acting out' (or exploding) an oppressive aspect of destructive energy, and being victimised as 'acting in' (or imploding).[7] When we identify as victims, we tend to internalise offending by carrying negative self-beliefs and allowing others to disrespect and devalue us, and when we identify as offenders we tend to externalise victimisation by denying others' worth and unfairly blaming them. This is the basis of many social power games. Keep in mind that destructive energy is not necessarily oppressive, as death is part of Earth's cycle and violence and trauma are necessary for some of our growth and development.

EXERCISE

Most of us have a tendency to be hard on ourselves and excuse others, or to blame others and avoid personal responsibility. Do you have a tendency to internalise or externalise, to act out or act in? Do you behave differently in certain environments (for example, at work or home) or with particular people (for example, family)?

Our individual power is based on our ability to wield, carry and channel energies – like a baby's crying causing everyone around to turn towards them. There's also a lot of power in repetition; for example, nearly everyone on the planet knows what a christmas tree is even if they're not Christian. In Indigenous science, our individual power is rooted in our ancestry (of land, lineage(s) and spirit). Dr Apela Colorado says: '[P]ower comes from the ancestors to heal bones through touch within a few minutes, to heal the environment, to travel to the stars.'[8] Most of us are carrying too much trauma and other wounding to experience that depth of power regularly, but we can intentionally engage in a lifelong process of continually becoming aware of our power across all areas of the medicine wheel and using it to embody our values.

This process requires us to be willing to confront power dynamics that feel oppressive or imbalanced. One way to do that is by healing power dynamics between peoples, between peoples and lands, and between peoples and non-humans. In relationships of balanced power dynamics, no one has existential power over any other being. In order to heal imbalanced power dynamics, try the exercise on the next page.

EXERCISE

Ground and centre yourself. Visualise a person you feel out of balance with, where the power dynamic doesn't feel right. Set the intention for a healthy power dynamic between you. You may wish to visualise the other person's face. Breathe deeply. You may feel some energy entering or leaving your body, and in your third eye you may see energy exchanging. You may wish to do this to heal dynamics between yourself and a group of people, yourself and a place, or yourself and a non-human being.

Expand this exercise further by calling in ancestors who are willing to heal power dynamics. Start by setting an intention for healthy power dynamics between your lineage(s) and the land you live on. Expand to include other lands, peoples and non-humans as you intuit would be healing.

Patience

WEEK BEGINNING: _____

SEASON: _____

In week 19 we considered the relationship between synchronicity and timing in Indigenous science. Implicit in this understanding of time is the importance of patience. Apalech scientist Tyson Yunkaporta says when you want to learn something, 'You have to show patience and respect, come in from the side, sit awhile and wait to be invited in.'[1] Similarly, Ts'msyen scientist Jo-Anne Chrona explains that 'learning happens when a person is ready for it', which is different for each individual and is based on 'cultural values of collaboration and taking the time needed to develop consensus'.[2] While consensus building takes longer than majority rule voting, it is an inclusive and relational process that allows each person to learn from the other, resulting in everyone reaching agreement when they feel ready, rather than forcing a majority rule decision that creates winners and losers.

In many Aboriginal Australian languages is a concept of patience, right timing and waiting that doesn't directly translate into English. In the Western Arrarnta language of the central desert, the word *anma* is described as an 'active space of preparation', encompassing the concepts of 'waiting, giving space, waiting for the right time, not filling up all the space, being patient and waiting until the other person feels ready'.[3] Amazonian Indigenous medicine people similarly say that 'patience is of the utmost importance and healing will occur when the time is right'.[4] This may be of limited comfort to our modern minds, which are increasingly conditioned to expect instant gratification, but on a soulful level of being it likely resonates and makes sense. We know we can't rush a caterpillar out of a cocoon and into a butterfly any more than we can rush a six year old to be a mature adult.

Sioux scientist Ohiyesa describes patience as an aspect of the 'holiness of silence' along with self-control, courage, endurance, dignity and reverence.[5] We can see such values underlying modern political strategy among some Indigenous peoples,[6] such as the way the Anangu (the traditional owners of Uluru in the central Australian desert) waited many years for legal title and joint management of their lands, and then many more years for the power to end tourists climbing their sacred site.[7]

I realise that it can be hard to sit in pain, trust the process and wait patiently for the right timing before we act. For most of us, patience takes active effort more often than it involves passively passing time. We are no longer accustomed to sitting for hours waiting for an animal we want to eat to be close enough for us to spear it. I would describe right timing as clear action through synchronicity and flow states of being. It is as if we are compelled to act in a way that feels effortless deep down inside, even if on other levels our experiences are hard. In such a state of faith we are driven by a knowing bigger than our individual selves, playing our role in a cosmic drama as it unfolds. Spiritual ambition and other tricks block us from experiencing this, so it is wise to monitor Indigenous science data and seek feedback along the way to ensure that waiting is still called for, especially when we feel insecure.

EXERCISE

Reflect on patience in your own life. How much do you value a concept like anma? What blocks you from waiting for the right timing? When do you feel strong about being patient? What helps keep you occupied and distracted from discomfort when you need to practise patience?

Often we make agreements to ease our journeys, sometimes because we feel forced to by Western systems. It is important to have compassion about this and keep in mind that agreements can be revisited when circumstances change. As Hawaiian Elder Hale Makua reminds us, the paradox of change is that it is permanent and detours are inherent in life:

> You may seem to go off course; you are still on your way. Detours may even be necessary to ensure survival and success. You can only go as fast as the wind will take you requiring timing and patience. [Simply] notice where you are and who is on the journey with you and focus on the direction you wish to go. Allow the wind to carry you.[8]

I have seen a number of people block their flow and lose trust in the process of life by getting tricked with mental logic. It isn't very powerful to be familiar with something only intellectually. It is much more powerful to have experienced it fully: mentally, physically, spiritually and emotionally. This gives us the ability to deeply connect with people by sharing a heartfelt story from our own lives, and to have standing to speak about something with embodied authority. Consider the difference between someone speaking to you about childbirth who has had children of her own and has been present at the birth of many members of her family and community, and someone who has studied midwifery at university and attended a handful of births. The intellectual knowledge of the midwife might offer you some value, but stories of what the other woman has seen that relate to what you are going through will likely be more powerful medicine that resonates with your heart, not just your mind. And if someone has both of these skills – Indigenous and Western science knowledge – that may feel even more powerful.

EXERCISE

Remember a time when you allowed mental logic to block
you from experiencing something. What do you feel now,
looking back? Did it come up again in your life in another
form? Do you feel any regret or curiosity about it still?

Calendars

WEEK BEGINNING: _____

SEASON: _____

There are many ways of acknowledging seasons and cycles and measuring the passage of time. Since we're all familiar with the Gregorian calendar, let's start there. It was introduced in 1582 by Pope Gregory XIII to correct leap-year timing and align better with the date for the spring equinox, which is used to determine the timing of easter.[1] It is a solar calendar, meaning it follows the cycle of the sun. Solar calendars tend to be used by agricultural and empire-building cultures, including Christian, Berber and Tamil peoples.

A calendar based solely on the lunar cycle is, not surprisingly, called a lunar calendar. It may have 12 or 13 months in honour of the number of moons in a year, and cultures following this type of calendar include Islamic, Igbo and Yoruba peoples. Alternatively, a calendar that is based on both solar and moon cycles is called a lunisolar calendar. Because days, weeks and months are fixed, holidays determined by the lunar cycle fall on different calendar days each year. Cultures using a lunisolar calendar include Hebrew, Buddhist, Hindu, Chinese, Korean, Tibetan and pre-Christian Germanic tribal peoples. You may think that four seasons a year have been standard in European cultures, but the Old Norse calendar had only two: summer began in mid-October, and winter in mid-April.

Another type of calendar called a seasonal calendar is based on elemental (earth, air, fire and water), floral (plant) and faunal (animal) patterns throughout a year. The number and types of seasons are dependent on specific places, so even peoples that reside near each other may have different seasons, for reasons such as a river flooding during a wet time of year, a predominant wind that comes through a certain time of year, or a flowering plant or an animal that migrates across the land at a specific time of year.

Some cultures with seasonal calendars have corresponding sky-based calendars that are mapped alongside their land-based calendars, notating the relationship between changes in the night sky and changes in the physical landscape of a place. Aboriginal Australian and Pacific Islander cultures are known for having seasonal and corresponding celestial calendars that are place based. Recent collaboration between Western and Indigenous scientists has resulted in some beautiful depictions of seasonal calendars from Aboriginal Australian peoples.[2] Sometimes seasonal calendars are also referred to as weather calendars.[3]

EXERCISE

What calendar(s) are you familiar with? Do you pay attention to the cycles of the moon, even if you only use a Gregorian calendar? Do you follow the cycles of other celestial bodies like the planets' influence described in a type of astrology? Do you notice that certain plants, animals or weather phenomena occur at a certain time of year where you live? Reflect on how the calendar(s) we use affect(s) the way we experience seasons and cycles, and understand and measure the passage of time.

The wheel of the year is a common calendar used by modern-day pagans of European ancestry that is based on the equinoxes and solstices, and the half-way moments between them (called cross-quarter days; see the appendix) to mark changes on a four-season calendar[4] (While the word 'pagan' may make you think of someone who worships multiple gods, it actually refers to people 'fixed or fastened' to the land whose culture is indigenous to, or rooted in, a specific place.) A wheel of the year calendar is often embedded into a medicine wheel divided into four parts with the solstices and equinoxes at the edges of each part, and the cross-quarter days in the middle.

It is an empowering act of decolonisation and re-indigenisation to create a calendar that has meaning to you instead of simply following the Western Gregorian calendar with its nationalist, Christian and commercial holy days. So let's do it!

EXERCISE

Get some paper and coloured pencils (or however you prefer to draw). If you are not living on lands of your blood lineage, I suggest starting with the wheel of the year and building out from there, and adding important dates to you such as birthdays, anniversaries and other holy days. Consider using the template below of a wheel of the year calendar transposed over a Gregorian one.[5] (Cross-quarter days are marked as circles and lines mark equinoxes and solstices.) If you have a four-part medicine wheel, aspects of your wheel may be written in the upper open area, land-based cycles in the next area, and important dates below each month. Don't worry if you don't know some things. You can't do this wrong; you have a unique ancestry (of land[s], lineage[s] and spirit), and the way you celebrate seasonal, solar and/or lunar cycles can be your own.

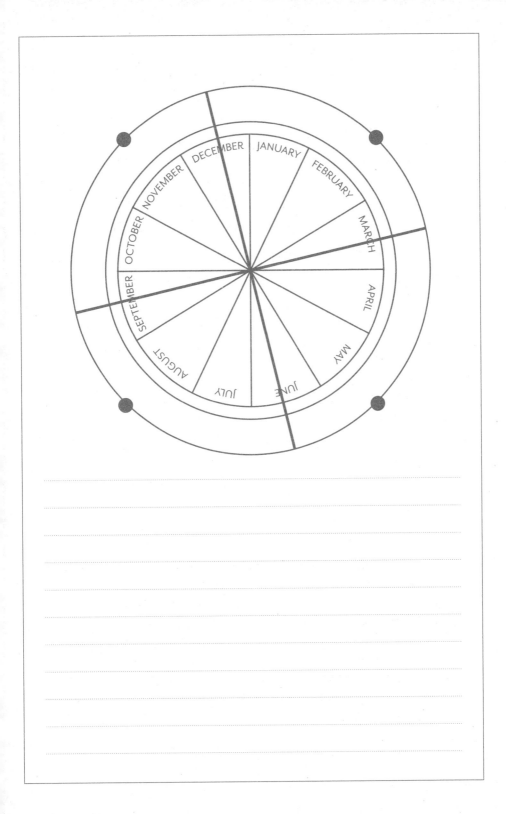

To give you some examples, in my calendar each of the four parts is associated with aspects of my medicine wheel. My direction of south represents the emotional, the water element, autumn, the colour red, the cycle of rebirth, mothering, a sacred mother mountain south of where I live called Gulaga, my Sumerian (Jewish) lineage and the date palm (a sacred plant). I am developing an understanding of a land-based seasonal calendar for Yuin country on the south-eastern coast of Australia where, for example, humpback and southern right whales migrate north to breed in autumn in May. I like to honour the international holy days of Earth Day, the International Day of Peace, International Day of the World's Indigenous Peoples and Martin Luther King Junior's and Nelson Mandela's birthdays. I also honour birthdays and death days as well as new and full moons and eclipses.

Listening

WEEK BEGINNING: _____

SEASON: _____

From an Indigenous science perspective, listening includes receptivity to messages from humans, as well as plants, animals, minerals, the elements, landforms, spiritual beings seen with the inner eye or in dreams or visions and even from stars and other celestial bodies. Through deep listening in prayer, meditation, journeying, fasting or dancing, Indigenous scientists listen with the same level of respect to a message from the movement of a falling rock or flow of a river as to the words or actions of another human.[1] As Tiwa Elder Beautiful Painted Arrow Joseph Rael says, 'For the true human, the first thing is to find out how to listen ... Seeing, and the eyes, were created so we could move into things and through things. The ear, on the other hand, was created for the art of giving.'[2]

When thinking about listening as a tool for the art of giving, it may be helpful to consider the concept of empathic listening. Empathy may be defined as 'mentally identifying oneself with an object of contemplation, and so fully understanding or appreciating it'.[3] I understand 'mentally identifying' to refer to an experience of momentary unity through shared lived experience, imagination and/or an open-hearted connection. An Indigenous scientific understanding of empathy is inherently relational, and the use of empathic listening for maintaining relationships and facilitating healing is found across cultures, from the Buddhist's loving kindness to the African philosophy of *ubuntu* and the Australian Aboriginal concept of *dadirri*.

Ubuntu may be defined as 'I am because we are' or 'a person is a person through other persons'. It was an underlying ethos of the South African Truth and Reconciliation Commission,[4] and Nelson Mandela explained it as individuals enriching themselves in a way that facilitates community spiritual growth.[5] And Ngan'gikurungkurr scientist Ungunmerr Baumann defines dadirri as follows: 'It is inner, deep listening and quiet, still awareness ... When I experience dadirri, I am made whole again ... In our Aboriginal way, we ... could not live good and useful lives unless we listened. This was the normal way for us to learn – not by asking questions.'[6]

Based on concepts like ubuntu and dadirri, empathic listening is an embodiment of values like respect, acceptance, inclusivity and love.

The power of empathic listening is that we more deeply see and understand our own experiences through witnessing and taking in the reflection of another, gain insight into collective experiences and more deeply experience our inherent interconnectedness with all of creation. Empathic listening is done through empathic dialogues with another human or non-human. To listen we must be open and receptive to different forms of communication, and knowing a little about our dialogue participant makes it easier to make sense of their messages. For example, when I am driving and a bird swoops close to my car to go across a street my first thought would likely be that there is a large predatory bird in the area, so the smaller bird is using the air and sound disturbance of my car as a cover to safely relocate. If I didn't know much about bird behaviour I might interpret this as a dramatic message from the bird for me.

There are many ways to engage in an empathic dialogue. Sacred circles, also called 'talking circles' or 'peace circles', are used in many Indigenous cultures around the world as ceremonial opportunities for empathic dialogues. When we sit in a circle without tables or structures in between us (except perhaps a small altar on the ground in the middle of the circle), we collectively embody a medicine wheel. Practising listening through being part of a sacred circle is not merely sitting in a circle talking to each other; it is a facilitated process that reminds us of our interconnectedness and supports us to feel safe to be open hearted and vulnerable. If being part of a sacred circle process interests you, you may be able to find one to participate in online or in person.

Another way to engage in an empathic dialogue is to spend time at a 'sit spot'. All that is involved in cultivating a sit spot is sitting still and being as present and aware as you can. The best sit spot is one that you are easily able to access, as going to the same spot over time strengthens our practice and familiarises other beings with our presence. Even sitting for five minutes at a time can make a difference to how we feel in our bodies, how interconnected we feel and how much space we have for communications from non-humans. And if you really want to practise empathic listening, it can help to spend time with your eyes closed or sit at night to focus more fully on listening without the use of physical sight.

EXERCISE

I suggest trying both of these exercises and noticing any differences you experience. Keep in mind it is best to do these regularly, even for a few minutes a week. Give yourself grace if it's hard to hear or feel past your own inner voices at first. As you cultivate more space for listening over time, you will notice a difference in daily life.

1. *Choose a spot in your home where you can regularly take time to sit in stillness and practise empathic listening. Make yourself comfortable enough that the experience isn't focused on physical feelings of uneasiness related to the way you are sitting. Open your practice by creating sacred space, such as purifying with some smudge or lighting a candle, then take a moment to ground and centre yourself. You may wish to set a timer for five or 10 minutes, or you may wish to sit until it feels right to stop. Notice your thoughts and feelings and any signs in your environment.*

2. *Choose a sit spot outside your home, ideally in wilderness, such as a backyard, park or beach that is easy for you to access. Make yourself comfortable. Open your practice by creating sacred space, and grounding and centring yourself. You may wish to set a timer. Notice your thoughts and feelings and any signs in your environment. Notice how birds and other animals change their behaviour when you sit for a while.*

WEEK

32

Story

WEEK BEGINNING: _____

SEASON: _____

We each carry many stories whose meanings influence our beliefs, values, thoughts, behaviours and paths in life. We may be aware of certain stories and beliefs that have deeply impacted us, such as biblical stories, fairy tales, cultural lore or proverbs like 'money is the root of all evil'. There is a saying from the Nhunggabarra people of Australia that 'the story owns the storyteller'. The idea is, whether we are consciously aware of it or not, we are attracting and repelling experiences and relational dynamics, as well as deriving meaning about them based on deep underlying stories.

Some stories may come from intergenerational traumas and other wounding from our families and communities, such as a story about white supremacy. Still others may be stories we learned to tell ourselves through lived experiences, which may be supportive (for example, 'I am good at cooking'), destructive (for example, 'Nothing I do is good enough'), and anywhere in between. It is often easier to become aware of stories we are telling ourselves, and experiences that led us to embed those stories and related beliefs into our lives. For example, a woman who moves interstate to care for her elderly parents may remember feeling pain as a child when she saw an elderly neighbour being neglected.

EXERCISE

Reflect on a story you tell yourself, a thought loop or belief
you are aware of carrying that feels destructive. Leave an offering
such as a flower or lit candle at your ancestral altar with an
intention or prayer for insight about how to let it go.

Some stories we internalised when we were young. Such stories often act as parables, teaching us culturally acceptable ways to behave and collective core values. With deep listening, we can re-member stories we took to heart when we were young and see their impact throughout our lives. For example, a woman who read Anne Frank's *The Diary of a Young Girl* as a teenager may become fascinated with Judaism, read more stories about it and end up decades later marrying a Jewish man and converting to the religion herself.

EXERCISE

Reflect on a story that deeply impacted your life. How do you feel about it now? How do you see the story differently after living with its influence on your life? What do you still appreciate about the story and its effect on your life?

Jungian scientist Clarissa Pinkola Estés says, 'Stories are medicine . . . embedded with instructions'[1] that guide us about how to live our lives. And with very deep listening, we can not only see stories and beliefs underlying large-scale recurring patterns in our lives, but start to understand how we formed a sense of identity through valuing some character traits and archetypes over others. Digging deep inside ourselves, we often find 'central myths' at the core of our being that define our life's path. Central myths differ by culture and context. Common central myths in Western culture include: the archetype of a transformative hero's journey,[2] as popularised by Joseph Campbell; the archetype of a saviour/martyr embodied by Jesus Christ,[3] and the fairy tale archetype of a damsel in distress.[4] Myths common throughout the capitalist world are: if you work hard, you will realise your dreams and become financially, socially and emotionally successful;[5] an individual has a right to the pursuit of personal pleasure and fulfilment;[6] and 'might makes right'.[7]

One of my central myths was based on a core belief about being a 'good person' from my Jewish mother, and a grounded example of that from my Frisian father's folklore through a story called *Sterntaler* (star money). The story is about a girl walking home from town and along the way passing people in need to whom she gives the food she bought, the basket she was carrying it in and the coat she was wearing. When she nears home, a Mother Earth figure called Frau Holle who controls the weather rains gold coins from the sky to reward her. The underlying belief I carry is to 'Give generously, and Mother Earth will provide what you need.' I still believe this, and it still serves me. And by reflecting on the dark side of this central myth, I realised that I needed to be more discerning about giving generously and have stronger boundaries to protect myself and ensure that my gifts were being honoured.

It is empowering to be consciously aware of the stories that 'own us' so we can hold them fully and enliven them wisely. Being aware of them also frees us from projecting them onto others in an attempt to see ourselves more clearly. I encourage you to explore central myths you carry to more deeply see your sense of identity and core values. In my experience it feels freeing, humbling, and ultimately brings peace as we more deeply understand the influence of central stories in our lives.

EXERCISE*

Create sacred space through purification, grounding and centring.
You may wish to be somewhere you feel safe and secure such as a sit
spot or altar. Make an offering and ask for insight into a central myth.
Be patient and sit with yourself as you settle into stillness and make space
for a central myth to emerge. Parts of your body will likely enliven with
energy. Feel into one of those places and do some deep listening to gain an
understanding about what it is carrying. You may have memories, thoughts,
feelings or other Indigenous science data emerge. Witness what arises.

*Reflect on dark and light aspects of the myth that comes up. How
has it shaped your identity? Your core values? How is this myth
and its teachings still serving you? What is not serving you? How
might you embody this myth in a more fulfilling way?*

....

....

....

....

....

....

....

....

*It is a hard-core process to change a central myth, but it can be done. If you feel
a desire to renounce a central myth altogether and let it go from your life, ask for
insight and guidance about how to do this through sacred ceremony. Once you
get clarity, do the renunciation ceremony with gratitude for the story and its
teachings. Be gentle with yourself, as you will likely experience feelings of terror,
existential crisis and annihilation when some of your sense of identity and core
values are transformed through the death/rebirth aspect of the earthly cycle.*

* This exercise was inspired by an exercise in Mary Mueller Shutan, *The Body Deva: Working with
the Spiritual Consciousness of the Body*, Findhorn Press, United Kingdom, 2018, chapter 11.

Culture

WEEK BEGINNING: _____

SEASON: _____

A creation story is a mythical seed from which a culture springs forth from the centre of a medicine wheel. Every culture teaches us our placement within creation and a social system through stories. Because creation stories are so foundational, they offer profound insight into how members of a culture perceive and organise the world. They 'connect past and present, clarify the meanings of important events, reaffirm core norms and values, and assert particular understandings of social order and individual identity',[1] and thus serve as a model for all of our behaviour.

Creation stories differ by culture, and the word *culture* is Latin for the 'act of worship' or a path of living that a group of people considers righteous. Culture describes what we cultivate in our lives. It is a metaphor for the seeds we plant and nourish, and those we consider weeds and remove; the parts of our world that we allow to be wild and untamed, and those that we consciously tend. It is a fundamental human need to be part of a culture, and creation stories are embedded beneath 'normal' or 'traditional' ways of being and doing, informing the core values and perspectives of a culture.

Many creation stories share the perspective of a divine being in a state of oneness creating life from darkness into light, often through sound or word. It is the most common form of creation myth and is found in cultures on all continents. An example comes from the Māori of New Zealand, with a creator being called Lo who was alone in stillness and in order to generate motion used words to call darkness to become light-possessing.[2] In North America, the Hopi creation story involves a being called Taiowa living in a void of endless space who creates a being called Sotuknang, who then creates form out of formlessness and molds life on Earth as we know it.[3] The Judeo-Christian creation story is also an example of this type of myth, of an infinite being creating life through the words 'Let there be light.' And the big bang theory of Western science is this type of creation myth too, of light arising out of the dark void of space and into physical form.

In addition to the first creation of life, cultural creation myths also describe the creation of the first humans. For example, the story of Adam and Eve in Judeo-Christian culture portrays the Earth as less of a home and more of a place to endure to earn a place in heaven and return to a blissful edenic state, and Eve as a blameworthy woman who caused humans to experience the hardship of earthly life.[4]

EXERCISE

Make a list of cultures you feel connected with. The list may include cultures of your lineages, Indigenous cultures of the lands where you live, work and/or were born and cultures you feel a connection or kinship with. Which cultural creation stories on your list are you familiar with? Take some time to research myths you don't know.

Using one of the myths, reflect on what it teaches you about core cultural values and about humans' placement on Earth and your social placement. How does this creation myth resonate with you? Do you feel any values conflicts with its teachings?

Since we 'develop as participants in cultural communities . . . [our] development can only be understood in light of the cultural practices and circumstances of th[ose] communities'.[5] One of the best ways to illuminate our own cultural values and norms is to place ourselves into a different cultural context. As any traveller can attest, we learn a lot about ourselves through the reflection of other diverse perspectives. These days many of us grow up navigating different cultural perspectives with very little travel in multicultural households and communities. And since it is exceedingly rare for a human culture to be so isolated that its stories, lands and traditions remain unchanged by colonialisation or globalisation, it is safe to assume that if you're reading this book you are likely carrying multiple cultural myths.

We wouldn't expect someone from northern Europe to have the same culture as someone from Australia, but when a bunch of people with northern European ancestry move to Australia (willingly and unwillingly), what does that mean for the culture of the people living on the land we now call Australia? For the majority of us who come from lineages with immigrants, slaves, refugees and/or forced migrations, our cultures have been disconnected from our lands of origin and affected by (forced and willing) cultural assimilation. In addition, unhealed traumas 'can seep through layers of culture and society in the manner of toxic chemicals eroding layers of earth',[6] distorting our cultural identity and even our core values and stories.

If you go back a few generations, how many ancestors of your blood lineage spoke your native language? Dressed in clothes like yours? Listened to similar music or did similar dances or art? Were taught similar stories about the right ways to live? Lived on the same land as you? Or ate foods native to the land where you live? How do we honour the complexity of our multicultural modern realities? One study found that just thinking about our ancestors and how they lived is beneficial to us,[7] so I invite you to do the following exercise as a small way to honour a culture in your life.

EXERCISE

Pick a culture you feel connected with and don't know much about. Learn a few words in the traditional language and see how you feel when speaking them. Put on some traditional music and see how your body wants to move to it, and eat some traditional foods and note your enjoyment (or not) of eating them. Spend time imagining how these cultural ancestors would have lived a few hundred years ago. What daily activities, traditions and ceremonies do you have in common? Is there anything you'd like to revive in your life today?

Non-human kin

WEEK BEGINNING: _____

SEASON: _____

Forester Peter Wohlleben wonders why, if we humans are really the most intelligent species on the planet, we work so hard to teach other creatures like parrots and chimps to speak our language rather than learning to chirp or hoot in theirs.[1] In Indigenous science we do learn to communicate with animals and plants in spiritual and practical ways, because kinship relationships include animals, plants, landforms, elements of nature, celestial bodies and spiritual beings. Cultures traditionally honour such relationships in different ways. One of the most familiar are totem poles carved by peoples of the Pacific north-western US and Canada such as the Haida, Salish and Tlingit. Totem poles encode much cultural knowledge, including historical events, lore and law and practicalities such as how to hunt a specific animal.[2]

Common Indigenous science traditions for honouring totemic and other non-human kin across cultures include: creating tree and/or rock altars outdoors; wearing animal skins and bird-feather headdresses; making musical instruments from animal skins and bones; ceremonial song and dance mimicking an animal; carving bones or tusks into beads or other jewellery; paintings and other art; festivals to honour an animal or plant at a hunt or harvest; and storytelling. It is helpful to note that the word 'totem' is used in different ways. Some people use it interchangeably with 'spirit animal' or 'power animal', though others distinguish between them.[3] Aboriginal Australians tend to use 'totem' to refer to animals connected with their kinship groups for which they are responsible as if they are protecting their own lives,[4] and to 'traditional lands' or 'my country' to refer to a landform or place with kinship relations.[5]

In Indigenous cultures, totemic relationships run through lineages, and individuals may acquire additional relationships through lived experiences. For example, the Gunditjmara people of south-western Victoria in Australia have two totems at the highest level of their kinship system, one for each moiety. Within each of those moieties there are additional layers of inherited totems based on someone's nation, clan and family, as well as marriage totems. People also have individual totems relating to their strengths and challenges.[6] All totems link people to places, air, water and specific landforms, so each Gunditjmara person has multiple totems and each is associated with laws and lore that person is responsible for learning and upholding.[7]

Many of us do not come from cultures with traditional kinship and totemic systems intact. I will share an example from each of my lineages. I know my family totem from my paternal lineage because it survived as my father's surname (and my middle name), which is German for 'swan'. Though much of our traditional knowledge has been lost over time, I know that the swan is associated with a medicine person or shaman. This is in part because the swan is the first bird to return to many Eurasian lands in the spring and the last to leave in the winter, so it is seen to move between the earthly and spiritual realms. There is also surviving cultural lore across Eurasia about shamanic shapeshifting 'swan maidens' that further illuminates this connection.[8]

Since swans are monogamous they are often also seen as symbols of love and loyalty, and their white colour tends to convey spiritual purity (like the white-feathered angels of Western culture). Black swans are more common in the southern hemisphere, and my understanding of Germanic lore is that their rare appearance in the northern hemisphere is a sign of unexpected change coming. I currently live in Australia in a small town with a black swan as its totem, and instead of feeling like the 'black sheep' of my family I feel like the black swan, the bringer of unexpected change.

On my maternal side, totemic relationships have been hidden over many generations of practising Judaism and have taken quite a bit of digging to uncover. Since I can remember, I have enjoyed dates and found them particularly nourishing. The first time I saw date palms growing I stared at them for hours through the window of a train. Years later, I intuitively started leaving a date on my personal altar and offering them at my ancestral altar. It is hard to describe the depth of resonance I felt when I learned that on my ancient Sumerian ancestors' country, 'The Iraqi palm tree . . . is like the American buffalo to the Indians – they use every bit of it.'[9] There is even an ancient Sumerian saying that has been incorporated into a modern cookbook by an Iraqi-American artist titled *A House with a Date Palm Will Never Starve*.[10]

Further, I learned that most date palms have long thorns and that you have to be careful when harvesting the fruit, leaves and wood from them to avoid injury. This also resonated with me, as I have a challenging relationship with this lineage and have for some time described my relationship with my mother as being consistently poked by a cactus spike in her presence. I now know that this is my moiety totem in that lineage, and other totems may become known to me over time.

Whether we have totemic connections with non-humans or not, we can still honour them and consider them our relations, such as through the exercise on the next page.

EXERCISE

Choose one of your totems or a non-human you experience a strong connection with and take a moment to reflect on it. What kind of environment does that being need to thrive? How does it behave? What are its essential qualities? What connections do you see and experience? How does your sense of identity relate to it in an Indigenous cosmology? How do, or could you, honour it across all aspects of the medicine wheel (spiritually, physically, emotionally and mentally)?

Discernment

WEEK BEGINNING: _____

SEASON: _____

As Diné (Navajo) Elder Wally Brown says: 'You can never conquer fear, it's always going to be there . . . Walking in beauty involves encountering fears, physically, emotionally, mentally and spiritually, and getting beyond them, so we can have joy, happiness, confidence and peace in the four areas of our being.'[1]

By 'getting beyond' our fear, Wally is referring to developing discernment. Fear is a challenging energy to be with, and it's one of life's beautiful paradoxes that we can learn to be safe with our fears, creating space and understanding about how and when to act even when we feel terror flowing through us. In Western culture we talk about emotional intelligence (EQ) and mental intelligence (IQ), but rarely about physical or spiritual intelligence. Physical intelligence is related to our relationship with our environment, as well as our own bodies. And spiritual intelligence has to do with our capacity to hold paradoxical energies, our ability to access altered states of consciousness and skilful use of Indigenous science data.

I am using the word 'discernment' instead of 'judgement', because judgement is often linked with negativity but 'sound judgement' is similar to skilful 'discernment'. I think of discernment as a muscle more than a practice, because it inevitably gets regular workouts through our life experiences. We are wise to work out the muscle so it's in good shape to navigate inevitably testing moments in our lives. Discernment is grounded in our desire to uphold core values (week 3) and will help us strengthen our boundaries (week 21). One of the best ways to work out this muscle in everyday life is through the following exercise. It is easiest to do this exercise when you have a conflict, challenging emotion or thought loop to work through. It is most powerful when done in the moment of a heightened fear response, if you are able.

EXERCISE

Reflect on a recent experience of fear and other intense thoughts and/ or feelings. When you have an instance to work through, go into that energy and ask yourself 'Is it mine?' Breathe through any discomfort and await a deep inner clair response. You may hear an inner voice or have a feeling or sense of knowing, or you may see an image that clarifies this question.

If you realise that it isn't yours, that it is ancestral trauma or a projection from someone else, set an intention to let it go and ask your wise inner self for guidance about how to do that. If you realise that at least some of it is yours, ask yourself, 'What per cent of this is mine?' Set an intention to let go of what is not yours, and ask your wise inner self for guidance about how to do that. For what is yours, you may wish to ask your wise inner self what the underlying fear, belief or myth is, and for any guidance about working through it. You may also wish to ask your ancestors for guidance with this or seek wise counsel from people you trust.

In Western culture, black and white thinking abounds in terms of apportioning responsibility. We are either guilty or innocent, or we share the blame 50/50. It is very hard for most of us to apportion responsibility outside of that 0/100 or 50/50 framework. Yet most real-world conflicts are complex, involving multiple parties with each bearing a proportion of responsibility. Taking responsibility for where we have some power doesn't excuse others from destructive behaviour.

For example, as a young woman I sometimes wore tight clothes and short skirts. Though I understand the importance of wearing what makes one feel good, I did not feel good or empowered having to process so many men's sexual projections (and women's jealousy projections) while walking around. I felt deeply uncomfortable, as it triggered wounds of previous sexual violence. So I started modifying my outfits, pairing a tighter top with a longer skirt and carrying a sweater or wrap to cover up when I felt overly exposed. I still experienced some uncomfortable projections, but those choices helped me feel good about what I was wearing as well as empowered to protect myself from many uncomfortable projections. I did not feel responsible for the projections other people were making, but since I seemed to be triggering people, I felt some responsibility to protect myself. Perhaps in an ideal world we would all be so self-aware that I wouldn't have needed to deal with such projections, but that was not my reality. I have since grown to more deeply value modesty and embed that into my values.

Another way to strengthen our discernment muscle is embodied in that story: try something and see how it works, then adjust as need. Years ago, I heard an interview with someone who had been in an abusive relationship for a long time, and he said that one of the most empowering things he did to heal was to give himself no longer than a day to make a big life decision, and no longer than an hour to make a small life decision. By holding himself to these timeframes, he limited his anxiety about making the 'right' decision, increased his empowerment about making a decision himself and increased his discernment muscle (as well as his ability to give himself grace) by experiencing how well his decisions turned out. Even when something went really poorly and didn't turn out how he had hoped, he said he felt a sense of pride that it had been his decision and knew he would learn from it. This strategy may not work for you, but the underlying idea is empowering for your discernment muscle. Sometimes we overthink, overanalyse or overconsult others for advice, and the best thing to do is take a step in a direction and await feedback from the universe.

All discernment relies on some foundational knowledge. When we are confused, lost or tricked, we have poor information with which to discern what to do. This is another reason why grounding and centring practices are so vital. If we think about it in terms of intelligence, if I don't have much physical intelligence about my environment then I won't have much to go on when trying to discern where to set up camp. I will have to rely on knowledge from other environments, and I may learn the hard way that camping near a stream kept me close to water but that the water level rose more than I expected, or that the trees providing shade had branches that easily snapped in heavy winds. This is why local Indigenous knowledge is so valuable.

EXERCISE

Do you know how to survive a few nights in the wilderness environment where you now live? Could you find and/or build shelter, get water, make fire and otherwise keep yourself warm and forage for food? If not, empower yourself with some knowledge and connect with the Indigenous ancestors of those lands.

Forgiveness

WEEK BEGINNING: _____

SEASON: _____

ome years ago while working with practising Jews and Christians, I realised the underlying process many of them were continually going through: judge an act as righteously right or wrong, confront moral failings within themselves and others, then forgive and let go by giving anger to a higher power. The depth of potential existential judgement is so intense (for example, eternal damnation and social ostracisation) that it can be very hard for people to acknowledge 'wrong' behaviours. I have experienced numerous instances of trickery of someone intending to forgive and let go (or deciding to avoid an issue), resulting in hurtful and confusing passive-aggressive behaviours. Often the underlying issue emerges years later after so much resentment has built up and trust eroded that the relationship becomes very hard to repair.

I was taught this judgemental process by Jewish family members, and had it reinforced by community members while growing up. I am thankful that another process was also taught to me by some Frisian ancestors: the process of accepting. I became consciously aware of this process as an adult when I worked with Tom Lake (now retired), who founded the International School of Shamanism on the foundational process of 'unconditional love and acceptance'. Though it may at times seem more painful in the moment, I find loving acceptance brings me immeasurably more ease and peace than judging. I then discern what, if anything, I need to say or do when I experience hurt or realise I have caused hurt in another being. I remember Tom told me once that even when he doesn't think he's done anything wrong, if someone tells him that his actions have hurt them he chooses to apologise because it is not his intention to hurt anyone. I appreciate the humility in that, and that it also helps hurting hearts to remain open to an ongoing relationship.

A common misconception is that a process grounded in acceptance means we make excuses for concerning behaviours. That is not my experience at all. In fact, while working among Aboriginal Australians in the Northern Territory I heard lamenting from many community members about how Western ways have eroded their traditional forms of justice, and created more intense and seemingly never-ending conflicts. In many Indigenous Australian cultures, when someone broke a traditional law, a member of the aggrieved family would ceremonially spear a member of the offender's family. This ceremony created an opportunity for everyone to accept what happened, because the aggrieved party could admit wrongdoing and face a consequence that would then restore their social place in the community, and the offended party could act as a channel for spiritual retribution. This is referred to in English as 'payback'. The spearing could hurt or kill someone or it could miss them altogether, and the outcome was accepted as the will of the spiritual realm. Once the ceremony was done the issue was let go, and relationships were restored.

Now that the Western justice system has criminalised the payback ceremony, many Aboriginal people in the Northern Territory seem to struggle to reach forgiveness with their Indigenous science of justice. I heard about someone who had been in prison for years due to 'Western justice' who was released and immediately had to face spearing if he wanted to see his family and community again. I heard about family members of an offender being beaten up until someone agreed to be speared in place of the offender in prison. I heard about decades-long violent feuds involving multiple generations where many people didn't even know how the feud had started, but no one felt justice had been satisfied. I even heard about someone trying to sue someone else for using sorcery against their family as payback instead of spearing.

Whether a spearing ceremony resonates with you or not, it was working for these peoples for many thousands of years. Their shared understanding of the world, its laws, and the intervention of the spirit realm supported people to admit and face consequences for 'wrong' acts and then reach a space of collective forgiveness and letting go of the issue. For me, such a justice process accepts that being human inevitably includes engaging in some wrong acts. In traditional Indigenous justice processes it was very rare that anyone was seen as unredeemable, and even if they were it tended to be seen as someone's spirit being overcome by a disease such as Wetiko rather than a failure of their individual moral character. We are all influenced in our sense of self by stories and projections from others, and I encourage you to consider how you feed this in the following exercise.

EXERCISE

Reflect on someone you dislike and feel some aversion towards, whether it is someone you know or a historical figure like Hitler and fill in the blank: 'They are . . . .' Consider the meaning of saying someone 'is' a trait such as 'evil' or 'too selfish'. Is that their identity in your eyes? Do you judge it? How might you be hurting them and yourself by holding these stories and projecting that onto them?

Though we may not be able to ceremonially heal with the people who hurt us or people we have hurt, we can do spiritual ceremonies on our own to change the way we hold people and what we project. Shifting our perspective requires us to hold paradox and avoid binary and judgemental thinking. In Hawaiian culture people use 'Ho'oponopono, the traditional conflict resolution process . . . [to] create a network between opposing viewpoints . . . that allows dualistic consciousness to stand while becoming fully embodied by the ecstatic love of Aloha.'[1] In Hawaiian science, illness is caused by breaking spiritual law and requires the offender, aggrieved and their entire families to forgive themselves and each other, and seek forgiveness from the spirit realm before the illness can heal.[2] A traditional Ho'oponopono ceremony has been adapted for outsiders to practise forgiveness by Hawaiian kahuna (healer) Morrnah Simeona and her student Ihaleakala Hew Len.[3] Though these teachings have been criticised as deviating from tradition, I find one of the basic elements useful and include it as part of the exercise below.

EXERCISE

Ground and centre yourself and create sacred space. Bring to mind someone who has hurt you. Imagine that person's face and see them saying the following to you in your mind's eye: 'I love you. I am sorry. Please forgive me. Thank you.' If it feels okay, imagine saying the same phrase back to them. Be with any feelings that arise.

Next time you feel hurt by someone close to you and are ready to make up, consider doing some eye gazing and saying these four sentences to each other. Notice how you feel.

WEEK

37

Conflict resolution

WEEK BEGINNING: _____

SEASON: _____

Conflict resolution in Indigenous science is focused more on relationships and processes than reaching an agreement about a specific issue between particular people. Indigenous science considers conflicts to include many people across non-linear, cyclical time, so that non-human kin and ancestral spirits are also involved.[1] Consider the following statement from an Ojibway community called Hollow Water: 'Our tradition, our culture speaks clearly about the concepts of judgment and punishment. They belong to the Creator. They are not ours. They are, therefore, not to be used in the way that we relate to each other.'[2] This deepens our work on forgiveness in week 36, encouraging us to accept and let go of all judgement.

One of the most harshly judged behaviours in Western culture is child sexual abuse. Western scientific research has found that people who engage in sex offending tend to: lack empathy and intimate relationships; have an exaggerated negative self-image and a tendency towards mental manipulation; have identity and boundary confusion; be emotionally immature; have strong sexual-interest; and engage in self-punishing and obsessive-compulsive behaviours.[3] How can we help people with such wounds to heal and thereby improve community safety and well-being?

Hollow Water offers an example, as they have been working for over a decade with the perspective that a sex offender is not a 'bad' person.[4] 'He's always going to be here. His kids are here. Don't give up on this person. Keep at him until [he] understands that our focus is to one day have a healthy community.'[5] They don't 'sit in judgement'; they work to 'find ways of changing his behaviour, changing his lifestyle, and of supporting him . . . [using] kindness, honesty, caring, sharing and faith . . . [to] bring [him] back into balance'.[6] In one Western science study, after 20 years the sex offender recidivism rate in Hollow Water was six times lower than the Canadian average.[7]

Conflict resolution is approached similarly among many Indigenous cultures. For example, the Navajo have a concept of 'solidarity' based on an offender reconciling relationships with self, family, community, nature and the cosmos. This solidarity is also based on a deep emotional bond between people called *ké* that teaches the Navajo to 'always treat people as if they were your relative'.[8] Dispute resolution processes among many Indigenous cultures include the use of circle ceremonies. Sacred circle ceremonies are a communal embodying of the medicine wheel where 'people are safe within its fold', and everyone is 'welcomed and openly received' and can engage in 'honest communication from the heart'.[9]

Yet just because we are part of a communal circle does not mean that we have an equal level of intimacy with all people, or all beings, within the circle. Being in a sacred circle means we make space for each other to exist and express our gifts. Consider this quote from Western animist spiritual teacher Mary Mueller Shutan: '[P]eople who tend to be attracted to Animism are often good-hearted [and] wish to be kind to everyone and everything . . . [but] part of an Animistic practice [is] reclaiming . . . parts of ourselves that can defend ourselves and our homes . . . that can pounce and prey and track and growl . . . without guilt and . . . moral apprehension.'[10]

She gives an example of someone who has a wasp nest in their house asking about a gentle way to remove it. Her response is, why are you trying to be gentle with a wasp that could sting you and, if you are allergic, even kill you? It is important to set boundaries to keep ourselves safe. That doesn't mean going around trying to exterminate all wasps in a genocidal manner; it means teaching the wasps they can't build nests in your home space. It means some things are worth fighting for.

Fighting (or competing) is one approach to conflict resolution; other approaches include collaborating, compromising, accommodating and avoiding. Different situations call for different approaches, and each of us has our own preferences and discernments about what approach to use when. For example, if a respected Elder offers counsel that doesn't resonate you may decide that avoiding is best because it feels too disrespectful to outwardly disagree, though you will not follow their advice. Compromising may be the best approach when you and your partner both want to spend the household budget on different things, so you each give and take a little since the resources you have are limited, and accommodating may be what you choose when your child insists on wearing an outfit you don't think is warm enough. You may just let them wear it and take a jacket in case they need it.

Something to keep in mind when avoiding conflict is whether by doing so you are internalising a war within yourself. When I avoid a conflict but over time it keeps coming up inside me, I find that I need to stop avoiding and act. That may involve telling my story, creating art to express my emotions, doing something ceremonial to let it go or supporting others with a similar struggle.

EXERCISE

Which conflict resolution approach(es) do you tend to use: competing, collaborating, compromising, accommodating and/or avoiding? Reflect on a conflict in your life. How long have you been in it? Which approach do you want to use to resolve it? What is preventing resolution? (If you wish to talk with someone and don't feel it would be productive, consider 'talking' in a spiritual way like writing a letter and burning it.) Act on your insight and try to resolve it. How does that feel?

WEEK

38

Anger

WEEK BEGINNING: _____

SEASON: _____

We tend to see anger in a pretty binary way: either someone's anger is justified due to moral outrage based on breaking social (that is, Judeo-Christian) values, or someone should forgive or express their anger another way to avoid being abusive. In Indigenous science, anger is held in a more complex way as a basic human emotion that, though volatile, has the potential to teach us many lessons, including:

- ⊙ core values that we feel are worth fighting for
- ⊙ when we feel passionately about someone or something
- ⊙ when our boundaries have been crossed
- ⊙ our sense of injustice at ethical and moral failure
- ⊙ where we feel safer expressing anger than other emotions such as sadness
- ⊙ that we have been tricked and were playing the fool or acting entitled
- ⊙ where we are subconsciously carrying Judeo-Christian/mainstream values.

Shamanic teacher Tom Lake taught me that wishing our anger away is wishing our passion away, which is very self-destructive. Anger is a fiery emotion. It gives us energy to act, such as to set a boundary, advocate for a cause we care about or express through art or music. It's helpful to practise giving grace to ourselves and others when we use our angry energy less skilfully and are triggered into childlike screaming. Since it is often easier to remember feeling ashamed about being angry, I invite you to do the exercise on the next page to consider your relationship with anger in a more positive light.

EXERCISE

Reflect on a situation where you feel that your anger served you well. How did the anger feel? How did you use the energy of the anger to act? What do you see as a positive value of your anger?

Many of us feel angry when our sense of injustice is triggered. If we avoid quick judgement and dismissal of the person who committed the injustice and sit with the emotion a little longer, we can use acceptance and compassion to unpack on a deeper level why we feel so angry about the situation. We can use the anger to become consciously aware of core values that we feel are worth fighting for and boundaries that we need to maintain to feel healthy and safe. We can also see where we might be carrying judgement so we can shift that into acceptance instead.

For example, if I feel angry about another Aboriginal Australian dying in police custody, I may need to first do something to express the energy before being able to do any unpacking. I might yell out, stomp my feet, throw the newspaper I'm reading onto the floor or go outside and hit a punching bag. Once I've expressed the raw energy, I might reflect on my own or talk to a trusted friend about my reaction. Usually anger spurs us to do more than just vent or express the raw emotion. Anger tends to repeat, and even escalate, until we act on the core issue(s) triggering it.

So I may donate to a non-profit working to keep Aboriginal people out of prison or send an op-ed into my local paper. Or I may realise I am too judgemental of the police to write an op-ed that would have enough compassion I could be proud of it, so I might do some research on policing, or even sign up for a ride-along to increase my compassion and understanding for them. Then if I write an op-ed or do other social justice activist work I can have increased confidence that I will not be judging the police, but seeing them with dignity and respectfully calling out concerning patterns of collective behaviour. These may all be productive uses of my anger, and the next time I see a headline about an Aboriginal person who died in custody I may still feel angry, but it will likely feel less intense and volatile than the previous time before I had unpacked why I felt angry and then acted on that wisdom.

Internalised anger tends to create dis-ease. Some years ago I watched two beloved people (my father and my best friend) succumb to cancer that seemed to be based on internalised anger, causing them to self-destruct. There is some truth to the saying that carrying anger is like trying to poison someone else by poisoning yourself. But there is a difference between never being angry (which is unhuman) and working productively with our anger so we don't feel compelled to deny that it's there. When we remain aware, we can express the energy and act to uphold our integrity.

Anger that has built up over time can be challenging to work with, but we can express the raw energy and keep acting on what we learn as we chip away at the layers. For example, in order to survive childhood abuse, I internalised a lot of anger in the form of resentment. Some of the raw energy felt best expressed through grieving, some through intentionally destroying power objects (week 7). Other energy needed to be yelled or growled, and I found that my car was a soundproof place to safely let out some screams without scaring people.

My actions also included: expressing the anger through artistic means such as poetry or painting or dance; talking with someone I trusted and being witnessed and validated in the core values and morals underlying my anger; setting boundaries with people who treated me disrespectfully; and practising compassion and empathy through surrogate dialogues with people who had abused children to ensure I wasn't judging anyone. I did the forgiveness exercise from week 35 and visualised someone apologising to me, and I wrote letters in angry, harsh handwriting that I ceremonially burned or flushed down the toilet.

It is also worth considering how different cultures express and suppress anger. Some cultures consider expressing anger to be taboo, childish or a sign of emotional dysregulation and weakness; other cultures teach that men should express anger more than any other emotion, especially sadness or fear, which are signs of weakness.

Indigenous cultures like the Inuit use traditional fearful stories to prevent children's dangerous behaviours, and dramatisations to allow children to practise regulating anger. One Elder explains, 'If a child is hitting others, the mom may start a drama by asking: "Why don't you hit me?" . . . "Ow, that hurts!" she might exclaim . . . [and] emphasize the consequences by asking . . . "Don't you like me?" . . . [to get] across the idea that hitting hurts people's feelings, and "big girls" wouldn't hit.'[1]

Grief

WEEK BEGINNING: _____

SEASON: _____

My healings, awakenings and navigations of grief and loss have been quite intense for some years now. I have found that when we make space for all emotions, including our pains and sorrows, we honour ourselves and the spirits of those energies, which includes everyone else who carries them. This allows energies in our lives to flow – to be let go and emerge – without force, and a grounded power comes into being that further centres and strengthens us.

About seven years ago my father, mother figure and best friend passed away within a span of six months. My experiences of grief were different for each of them, which taught me a lot. With my father, I felt the deepest pain and sadness and cried the most. I mourned the loss of his presence and the relationship we had, and even more painful was mourning missed opportunities to connect and heal together while he was embodied. I have found that working with him as an ancestral helping spirit has been very powerful, and I heard him communicating with me soon after he passed. He regularly visits me in dreams and sends signs to support me, and many years after his death I feel that our relationship is better now than when he was alive. It feels more whole and authentic.

With my mother figure, my childhood nanny, when she passed I felt some sadness and a longing to have known her better as an adult. I felt there was a little left unsaid that she has since communicated to me in spirit, allowing me to see her more clearly and hold her more fully. Her death prompted me to revive a relationship with her daughter, and though we are not close our dynamic feels very caring and kind.

And with my best friend, I felt there was very little left unsaid or undone, as we had fully and authentically enjoyed our relationship while she was alive. My main experience at her passing was a longing for companionship, a big space she left to fill. I experience her as a helping spirit more in the background than my father, with gentle nudges and subtle signs about directionality and choices in my life.

When we grieve, it can help to remember that the depth of pain and loss we feel is related to the depth of connection and attachment we had with someone, and that grieving is a way of honouring the relationship. It can also help to remember that being alive means being open to experiencing emotions that feel more and less pleasant; that it's preferable to live with passion and deeply feel than to be detached, dissociated and numb. As Tiwa Elder Beautiful Painted Arrow Joseph Rael says, 'You have to go through separation before you can go through reunion.'[1] Grieving is part of the process of death transitioning into rebirth in the Earth's cycle, as our relationship changes form from physical to spiritual intimacy.[2]

There are many causes of grief in addition to a loved one leaving their body. Some of the hardest griefs in my experience, which many of us struggle to honour and give time and attention to, are caused by lost dreams and desires. For example, if you really wanted to have a child by the time you were 40 and find yourself celebrating that birthday without a baby or even a partner, you may feel a deep grief that your dream was not fulfilled. You may even feel regret, which is one way we carry grief about something not done or done in a way that we don't feel good about. Regret is a corrosive energy that eats us up inside, bitter and unpleasant. I offer the exercise below to help you process and transform that energy.

EXERCISE

Set an intention to work through a regret. See what arises into your awareness. Is that dream or desire still viable? Is it still important to you? If you answered 'Yes' to both questions, make a commitment to value yourself and your dream or desire enough to revive it. Take a moment to put more faith into this dream or desire. Then ask what step you can take towards fulfilling it? What support do you need?

If you answered 'No' to one or both questions, ask your wise inner self and/or your ancestors for guidance about a ceremony you could do to let it go. How would it feel to free up this energy?

Many of us also carry intergenerational and cultural grief. At our core, we humans are tribal and familial, and if like me you grew up with abuse and/or neglect, then aspects of life that were desecrated or neglected may need to be grieved as a way of honouring how much we value them. For example, there is a sacred reciprocity in the cycle of a parent raising a child, and then a child supporting a parent in their old age. I feel I have been denied this experience because I was raised with abuse and neglect, and also because my efforts at reciprocal caretaking were not valued and well received. I experience loss and grief around this. Sometimes I need to cry to express the raw emotion, talk to a confidant and be witnessed in my pain. Other times I may need to express myself through art such as poetry. Then, like with anger, once I have expressed the raw energy, I feel more clarity about acting on it. I may spiritually support family members by sending them blessings and leaving offerings at an altar, or support other people emotionally, mentally, spiritually and physically as surrogates for the sacred energy of parental caretaking that I still desire to express.

Much intergenerational grief has to do with loss of Indigenous science and cultural knowledge in our lineages, along with loss of ancestral lands and connections with those lands and Wetiko-like loss of spiritual strength. Oneida-Gaul scientist Dr Apela Colorado suggested to me a healing process based on contemplating a few questions, which I've expanded on in the exercise below.

EXERCISE

Ground and centre yourself and create sacred space. You may wish to leave an offering at your ancestral altar asking for support and guidance with this. Reflect on the following questions, one at a time, and make note of any insight that arises. You may wish to revisit these questions from time to time until this healing process feels complete:

⊙ What were your traditional cultural ceremonies?

⊙ How did you and your ancestors lose them?

⊙ What losses do you need to grieve so that modern authentic cultural ceremonies have space to revive in your life now?

WEEK

40

Narcissism

WEEK BEGINNING: _____

SEASON: _____

To reflect on narcissism, let's first consider its roots from Greek Indigenous science.[1] The concept comes from the tragic story of a forest nymph called Echo, who was punished for being overly talkative and only able to repeat what others said, and a handsome demi-god overcome by arrogance called Narcissus. He was so used to his good looks enchanting so many women that he treated them all quite poorly. When Echo fell in love with him and he rejected her, she mourned so deeply that she died of grief on a mountaintop and hardened into a rocky outcropping. Echo's friends prayed for retaliation, and the goddess of revenge, Nemesis, decided to punish Narcissus for his behaviour by making him fall in love with his own reflection. He saw himself in a pond and felt true love for the first time, but whenever he tried to reach out and touch his reflection it disappeared. He then felt the pain Echo had, of being unable to caress his lover, and he sat by the water in agony until his bones rotted into the soil and a flower (called 'narcissus') emerged where his body had been.

Echo gets left out of many discussions about narcissism, though her lack of self-identity and other-absorption is the perfect mirror for Narcissus's arrogant self-absorption. Echo's heart was shattered by his rejection, because she didn't have enough sense of self to recognise his terrible character. This is unfortunately a common dynamic in many relationships today, especially for those of us who are highly sensitive and empathic (week 20). If you're reading this book, chances are you can relate to Echo somehow, and I invite you to reflect on this through the exercise on the next page.

EXERCISE

Reflect on these questions: Have you been in a co-dependent relationship? Have you felt guilty about taking up space? Are you highly sensitive to negative feedback? Do you find yourself being a 'people pleaser'? Have you martyred yourself (overly sacrificed your needs for the sake of others) and later felt resentment about it? Do you find it easier to advocate for others than for yourself? Do you have a fear of abandonment? Do you find it easy to put others' needs before yours? Have you struggled to work out your needs in a relationship? Do you seek approval from others to feel good about yourself?

If you answered 'Yes' to any of the questions in the exercise it's likely you have some Echo wounds. Our Echo wounds tend to attract wake-up calls in the form of abuse, disrespect, not feeling good enough and being oppressed, suppressed, in our heads and disconnected from our bodies. It can be hard when we experience narcissistic abuse to realise that we are playing the role of Echo and to reflect on what we are responsible for, what we missed that got us into this painful relationship dynamic.

It may be harder for you to relate to Narcissus. Narcissistic wounds tend to attract wake-up calls in the forms of humbling experiences, disappointed expectations, childish and selfish behaviours, and 'Why me?' feelings of being picked on. Having narcissistic wounds does not mean we are necessarily bullying others without realising it; often we are bullying ourselves by carrying negative self-beliefs, allowing others to disrespect us and not standing up for ourselves, taking on things that aren't our responsibility and making excuses for others, seeking approval from others to sustain our self-worth, connecting with others to avoid feeling lonely or isolated and generally setting poor boundaries.

Often the first step towards retrieving lost soul parts is making space for tough emotions such as terror, anger, grief and distrust. It's as if we hid parts of ourselves underground for years in an effort at self-preservation. Then, as adults, when we set safer boundaries and begin digging and shining light into those dark spaces, those hidden parts of ourselves are understandably upset about being neglected and take time to heal and reintegrate so that we feel more whole. Guidance on this self-soul retrieval journey is the underlying foundation for some popular self-help books such as *The Artist's Way*,[2] *Women Who Run with the Wolve*[3] and *You Can Heal Your Life*.[4]

It is a mark of spiritual maturity to hold compassion for Echo and narcissistic parts of ourselves and others we are intimate with, while continuing to maintain healthy boundaries and a solid sense of self-worth. Apelach scientist Dr Tyson Yunkaporta explains that in Aboriginal Australian cultures the emu teaches about narcissism.[5] In the Dreamtime, emu damaged social relationships and lived arrogantly, selfishly and unsustainably, offering a vital to warning to people about how not to behave. In acknowledgement of this important teaching, Aboriginal Australian societies traditionally revolved around the emu's teachings, exemplified by the Dark Emu constellations in the Milky Way (week 9). Dr Yunkaporta explains: 'The basic protocols of Aboriginal society . . . include respecting and hearing all points of view . . . Narcissists demand this right, then refuse to allow other points of view . . . destroy[ing] the basic social contracts of reciprocity . . . until every member of a social group becomes isolated, lost in a Darwinian struggle for power . . . that destroys everything.'[6]

It takes courage, trust and faith to allow ourselves and others to be on journeys of remembering that who we are is undyingly eternal and innately whole, no matter what wounds we may be caught up in in the moment. As Dr Yunkaporta says, to heal these Echo and Narcissus wounds we have to go back to the basics of re-membering who we are: 'Narcissism is not incurable . . . Entire cultures and populations recovering from this plague have been left like orphan children with no memories of who they are, longing for a pattern they know is there but can't see . . . ask[ing]: Why are we here? How should we live? What will happen when we die?'[7]

Generosity

WEEK BEGINNING: _____

SEASON: _____

Despite our collective human disrespect of Mother Earth, she keeps generously supporting us to live and even tries to clean the water and air that we keep polluting and to regrow forests we have clear cut. Based on this foundation of generosity to all of creation arose teachings about Indigenous science about sovereignty, leadership and governance.

In Indigenous science, sovereignty emerges from the land beneath your feet. This is different to Western understandings of sovereignty that are top-down, where land can be 'claimed' in the name of a crown through empire-building processes. As Menominee scientist Ingrid Washinawatok explains: 'Europeans relegated sovereignty to only one realm of existence: authority, supremacy, and dominion. In the Indigenous realm, sovereignty encompasses responsibility, reciprocity, the land, life, and much more.'[1]

Cree scientist Sharon Venne explains that Indigenous sovereignty is 'related to our connection to the Earth and is inherent'.[2] From sovereignty flows governance. Instead of a majority-rule system that most modern democracies follow, Indigenous governance tends to be more inclusive and collective, more focused on the process than an outcome. Māori scientist Hirini Moko Mead says: 'Processes [and] procedures . . . need to be correct so that in the end everyone who is connected is enriched, empowered, enlightened, and glad to have been part of [a process].'[3]

Some basic principles of Indigenous governance include:

⊙ Egalitarianism, which refers to distribution of power and responsibilities. This is actualised through traditional laws about family and kinship obligations, responsibilities to uphold and pass on traditional knowledge and valuing social and gender-based cultural roles, as well as the roles of Elders and other leaders.

⊙ Flexibility refers to power being able to flow as needed and not being rigidly concentrated. For example, you may have in mind that many Indigenous cultures had a 'chief' or a 'counsel' of chiefs, but those leaders rarely made all major decisions for a community. More common among Indigenous cultures was traditionally a power structure such that a chief facilitated others into leadership roles, such that someone would lead during a hunting expedition, another during a ceremony and another during a crisis based on each person's expertise.

⊙ Balance is an important principle that relates to the fundamental notion of no individual having more power than the group as a whole. This is because group well-being is seen to lead to individual well-being, not the other way around. It also limits the possibility for corruption, so that if someone is misusing their power they can be removed and a new leader put in their place.

⊙ Inclusivity is commonly realised through collective decision-making that is usually done by consensus. This avoids power struggles and resentments that often build up in majority-rule governance systems. Consensus building also respects everyone's gifts and perspectives by taking the time to ensure everyone is okay with a major decision. The process taking longer than a majority-rule vote ensures that relationships are placed at the centre and demonstrates a trust in right timing if it takes a while to reach agreement.

⊙ Accountability in Indigenous governance flows downward from a leader to their community, family and non-human kin. To maintain a leadership role requires someone to sustain social support and respect.

⊙ Reciprocity is based in holistic, cyclical (non-linear) thinking, such that good governance requires leaders to engage in multigenerational, visionary thinking for future generations of humans and non-human kin when making decisions. This is very different to the short-term election cycle–based decisions many Western politicians contend with in order to survive in their roles.[4]

Mohawk scientist Taiaiake Alfred defines Indigenous leadership as the 'governance of change'.[5] And when we think of Indigenous leadership we tend to think of Elders, but old people do not necessarily become cultural Elders, though age and lived experience are generally respected across Indigenous cultures. Wakka Wakka and Wulli Wulli scientist Dr Tjanara Goreng Goreng defines an 'Elder' among Aboriginal Australian cultures as either an experienced and initiated person, or a person gifted (emotionally, physically, mentally and/or spiritually) who is an Elder in a particular space. She explains that the essence of sacred leadership is humility, though Elders also need skills in resolving conflict, creating unity, living cultural law and passing on traditions.[6] Western scholar Dr Robert Kegan similarly describes sacred leadership as a developmental journey through five levels of human consciousness as follows: ego-centric → socialised → independent → interdependent → sacred.[7]

And among Yup'ik people, leadership is about 'fostering a culture of alignment between individual values and goals and that of the group or community while also ensuring that there is space for individual expressions within that larger field'.[8]

EXERCISE

How do you embody generosity and sacred leadership in your life? Whom do you see as an Elder in human form or in spirit who is a role model for you?

WEEK

42

Gift economy

WEEK BEGINNING: _____

SEASON: _____

A nother aspect of Indigenous governance based on generosity is a concept called the gift economy. A market economy is based on exchange, how much we owe (based on lack) and are able to earn (based on social judgement). A gift economy is based on sacred reciprocity, how much we share (trust) and give away (based on abundance). Charles Eisenstein, whose work is built on Western, Indigenous and Buddhist sciences, describes a gift economy thus: 'A real community is a gift economy, where you can help your neighbour . . . and they don't pay you but they feel gratitude . . . they want to take care of you too . . . [I]n a gift culture the more you give, the richer you are, which is . . . the opposite of a money culture.'[1]

EXERCISE

Reflect on wealth and how you define it across the medicine wheel (spiritually, mentally, emotionally and physically).

Many Indigenous cultures traditionally embody the philosophy of a gift economy. For example, for the Kwakwaka'wakw people of Canada, the wealthiest people are those who are able to generously give away the most gifts in a potlatch ceremony,[2] which may be planned a year in advance and last for several days. During the ceremony the host distributes wealth among guests, traditionally including food, furs, canoes and, most preciously, songs. As Elder Agnes Axu Alfred explained: 'When one's heart is glad, he gives away gifts. Our Creator gave it to us, to be our way of doing things, to be our way of rejoicing, we who are. Everyone on earth is given something. The potlatch was given to us to be our way of expressing joy.'[3]

Potlatch ceremonies are ways of recognising social status, passing on inheritance and reconnecting with ancestral lineages (including with non-humans), celebrating life events such as marriages, naming ceremonies, traditional building-opening ceremonies and funerals, and an opportunity for someone to restore their reputation in the community after being shamed or humiliated.[4]

In some Indigenous cultures there is an element of competition built into the gift economy, turning it into a social status game that is a contrasting mirror to the capitalist social status game of accumulating. In the Mount Hagen area of Papua New Guinea, Indigenous people work for years to be able to give a *moka*[5] gift to another person, and the recipient then works to gather an even bigger moka gift to pay forward to someone else. A person who has given the biggest moka holds the positive social status of a 'big man', and a person who has debts he cannot pay has the negative social status of a 'rubbish man'.[6]

In the modern world, being part of a transactional, capitalist economy is compulsory for most of us to survive. Yet there are still ways we can embody gift-economy values.

The first principle of abundant giving is that we be filled up ourselves and have extra energy to give. This requires deep grounding in Mother Earth and in our ancestry so we have strong roots and are being nourished throughout our entire being. We have all hopefully experienced someone so brimming with kindness that we felt warm energy emanating from them when we were in their presence. Whether mentally, spiritually, emotionally or physically, we can only give to another what we are already containing. Once we judge or expect ourselves that we 'should' embody a certain state of being – such as being more kind – we are in lack. Being honest and appreciative about what we can abundantly give helps us avoid getting into lack.

Many acts of generosity without expectation of anything in return (not even a thank you) embody the spirit of a gift economy. Most spiritual traditions enshrine some values of a gift economy into their teachings, such as Jewish *tzedakah*, Christian tithing, Muslim *zakat* and Buddhist *dāna*, and some organisations such as Vipassana[7] meditation centres and Brahma Kumaris[8] talks and retreats operate entirely on participant donation. But when we volunteer or donate in the spirit of proving we are a 'good person', or to alleviate guilt, 'create good karma' or avoid social shaming for not giving a 'suggested donation', the spirit of the gift economy is eroded.

In my experience, embodying a gift economy in the modern world is challenging. Living in a way that aligns with sacred leadership and Indigenous governance values where many people uphold economies based in lack, capitalism and transactional exchange requires firm boundaries, strong skills of discernment, compassion and deep self-knowledge. To maintain integrity in the gift economy, we need to be willing to receive no money or expressions of gratitude for our efforts. At the same time, to prevent abuse we need to discern when to say 'no', to stop giving when it is no longer a gift or when someone starts trying to use or devalue our efforts instead of respecting them. I think of this as 'spiritual social work', and there are numerous opportunities for us to practise it daily. It may look like giving compassion to a person criticising our behaviour, or giving grace to a colleague struggling with narcissism.

In my life, the person in whose presence I felt the most abundance was a subsistence farm woman in rural Guatemala who had a condition causing her skin to change colour and peel off her face and body. She had such a strong, vibrant spirit she was emanating light, and to be in her presence felt joyful and peaceful. Though I have had dinner with billionaires, I consider her the wealthiest woman I have met.

EXERCISE

What do you experience an abundance of (spiritually, mentally, emotionally and physically), and how do you express and 'gift' that energy? Where do you experience lack (spiritually, mentally, emotionally and physically)? Ask your ancestors and wise inner self for guidance about acceptance-based healing of some energy in lack that is ready to shift.

Rest and stillness

WEEK BEGINNING: _____

SEASON: _____

Rest, relaxation and stillness are not things we can 'do', they are natural responses that we allow. They come into being when we stop creating tension and allow our energies to settle. In the modern world, many of us feel constant pressure to 'be productive' and struggle to see the value of stillness, resting only when we reach the point of exhaustion. But rest and stillness are important spiritual practices. We cannot be in the moment, connecting with creation and picking up signs and other Indigenous science data if our minds and bodies are too busy buzzing around. We need to be receptive to deeply listen, which requires us to value stillness and engage in practices to cultivate it such as dadirri (week 31).

Nap Ministry[1] founder Trisha Hershey, an African-American spiritual teacher, sees rest as a form of social justice resistance, a way to push back against capitalism, colonialism and ancestral exploitation such as slavery and forced wage work by embodying beliefs of 'This is enough' and 'I am worthy of rest.'[2] She reminds us that when we rest we are being productive and 'doing something' – we are honouring our bodies and giving our brains time to download and process information.[3] And 'rest' can occur in moments throughout the day from sleep to meditation or drum journeying, yoga, dance or other mindful movement, while enjoying a sit spot outside or sipping a cup of tea at a desk, while watching some silly brain-candy show or soaking in a bathtub.

EXERCISE

Note some ways that you already cultivate rest and stillness throughout your day. Then set an intention to value rest and stillness and reflect on what small act you could do to embody that value. You may wish to ask your ancestors or wise inner self for guidance. Keep in mind that our journey of reclaiming rest and stillness often starts with saying 'no' to something or someone else, and saying 'yes' to connecting more deeply with ourselves.

Yankunytjatjara Elder Bob Randall shares a teaching from his culture called *Kanyini*, the 'principle of connectedness through caring and responsibility that underpins Aboriginal life'.[4] Kanyini supports our embodiment of unconditional love by reminding us to be in caring relationship with our spirit, soul or psyche, our family and kinship (including non-human kin), our land or home or sacred Mother (where we're from and where we live) and our cultural creation stories and traditional knowledge. Bob explains how deep listening is required for us to embody Kanyini: 'We believe that [everyone] is given . . . the voice of the super-consciousness, and free will . . . When we hold the principles of Kanyini in our hearts and listen to the voice of the super-consciousness . . . all "our" needs are being met and all "their" needs are being met . . . All is in harmony and balance.'[5]

It is interesting to note that in this view, our individual free-will inner voice is louder than our inner voice connecting us with deeper levels of collective consciousness. So resting and stillness support us to see through the weeds of our own thoughts, desires and needs and connect with bigger energies.

EXERCISE

Set aside at least 15 minutes for this rest and stillness practice. If there is something you would like to let go of or get clarity about, you may wish to set an intention now. Then revisit the body relaxation video[6] and remain in that restful, still state for at least a few minutes afterwards. Can you discern the voice of your free will? Of your super consciousness? Of ancestors and loved ones?

Witness what emerges for you mentally, emotionally, physically and spiritually; for example, whether you have more space and awareness, or whether some emotion has come to the surface. Notice any insight that arises, whether an intention has manifested, and if you feel any different during the rest of your day.

Is this practice something you can continue so you may experience its benefits unfold over time?

Mindfulness practices are great ways to bring rest and stillness into our lives. Being in the moment brings us peace and helps us connect with the flow of life. Métis woman Jeanne Corrigal describes mindfulness as 'our Indigenous teaching of how to be in the world' and a way to re-member that 'there [i]s communication happening without talking' because we 'are completely connected to everything around'.[7] An ancestral altar practice (week 6), the gentle steps practice (week 4), a sit spot practice (week 30), forest bathing and connecting with a tree practice (week 7) are all beautiful ways to practise mindfulness through Indigenous science.

Another powerful way to cultivate rest and stillness is to spend time in silence with your eyes closed so there's nothing external for you to focus attention on. In the modern world silence is quite precious and can be hard to find – we may require the use of technology such as noise-blocking headphones or a sensory deprivation tank. But it is in silence that we see the reflection of our own busyness most clearly: even more so, I think, than being in the wilderness, where we are able to focus on the sounds of animals like birds singing or squirrels scurrying, or the sounds of wind whistling through tree leaves or water tumbling down a rocky stream.

EXERCISE

Reflect on what you need to create a safe, silent space for yourself, such as turning off your phone, putting a Do Not Disturb sign on the door of your room or using some earplugs. Create space that feels comfortable, cosy and safe for you to deeply dive into silence. If you have not done this much, allow your experience of silence even for a minute or two to be a success. If you have done this many times before, you may wish to visit a sensory deprivation tank or otherwise challenge yourself to experience silence even more fully.

Sit in the silence for as long as you are able. Witness what's happening within. Do you feel safe to rest? If not, why not? What is blocking you from resting in silence?

WEEK

44

Gratitude

WEEK BEGINNING: _____

SEASON: _____

Haudenosaunee tradition teaches us that peace requires gratitude. We are to be thankful for the living world. Our relationship to the Earth is the basis of our sustenance and our peacefulness ... [connecting] us to a perpetual process of creation, and ... [providing] all we need to be happy and healthy.'[1]

The Haudenosaunee is a confederacy of Native American nations brought together by the Great Law of Peace[2] over 1000 years ago, which has been transmitted on traditional wampu[3] belts ever since. This Great Law that brought the nations together is embodied in their Thanksgiving Address,[4] also referred to as Greetings to the Natural World, a prayer used to begin all communal gatherings that honours:

1. The People.
2. The Earth Mother.
3. The Waters.
4. The Fish.
5. The Plants.
6. The Food Plants.
7. The Medicine Herbs.
8. The Animals.
9. The Trees.
10. The Birds.
11. The Four Winds.
12. The Thunderers.
13. Grandfather Sun.
14. Grandmother Moon.
15. The Stars.
16. The Enlightened Teachers.
17. The Creator.
18. Other beings that may not have been named.

Each section of the prayer ends with a phrase translated into English as 'Now our minds are one' to affirm that the people intend to be consciously aware of their interconnection with each other and all of creation.

EXERCISE

Follow along with the video of the Haudenosaunee Thanksgiving Address[5] or any written version you can find online and read it aloud. Reflect on how this feels, and what life might be like if your community collectively opened gatherings in this way. Reflect on how you might integrate such expressions of gratitude for the natural world into your spiritual practice.

The principle of Kanyini introduced in week 43 relates to this gratitude for the natural world, as the 'key to Aboriginal wisdom is family. Treat every being as you would your mother, your sister, your father, your brother. All creatures – humans and other than humans – are family.'[6] A concept called *Ngurra-kurlu* shared by Warlpiri knowledge holder Wanta Steve Jampijinpa Patrick deepens our understanding. Ngurra-kurlu is translated as the 'sacred home within' and is symbolised by the Southern Cross constellation as a four-directional medicine wheel with Land at the centre.[7] Wanta Steve explains: 'Ngurra-kurlu is all about our place and sense of home. It consists of Family, Law, Land, Language, and Ceremony. Once we lose these five elements we become homeless people . . . We live in our home without really knowing how to look after it, and we run the risk of desecrating our home.'[8]

Many of us and our ancestors have had this experience of losing vital cultural knowledge, and many of us today are living on lands that we do not have deep ancestral connections with. But we can learn to be at home where we are, to connect with the Indigenous knowledge embedded in the land through our own efforts to build relationships there, as well as through knowledge sharing with Indigenous peoples. Wanta Steve further explains: 'The sounds of the land gives us words, the words gives us songs, the songs give us ceremonies, the ceremonies give us teaching, the teaching give [*sic*] us our beliefs, and the beliefs gives us our identity. The most important thing . . . [is] to learn to listen to this country.'[9]

What does it mean to listen to the land? First, just as we need to get to know our bodies, we must get to know the land, including our non-human kin and the local seasonal calendar (week 30). Spending time outside with the land, learning from Indigenous knowledge holders about the history of the land as well as from written records, supports us to build deeper relationships there and to feel more at home. As Potawatomi scientist Dr Robin Wall Kimmerer says, in a gift economy land 'has a bundle of responsibilities attached' to it and 'It is human perception that makes the world a gift.'[10] Consider this Indigenous science perspective about trees: 'Trees are our family . . . If we take their lives . . . we have to do it so that the generosity continues. If we build shelters with the wood, share the shelter with others; if we make fires for warmth, invite the whole family. Be generous like the trees.'[11]

EXERCISE

Set an intention to be aware of 'taking a life' from non-human kin, such as breaking branches to make a fire, moving rocks around your garden or picking fruit or veggies to eat. Reflect on how you honour these beings in sacred reciprocity, perhaps with words of gratitude, through land stewardship or in ceremony.

Belonging

WEEK BEGINNING: _____

SEASON: _____

Years ago, I heard shamanic practitioner Christina Pratt talk about belonging.[1] She said she used to think belonging came from her family, friends and community, but realised through working with Dagara Elder Malidoma Somé[2] that it comes from our roots – that is, our ancestors – not from living people. That set me on a journey of digging into my roots seeking deep ancestral and Earth-based belonging. At times on that journey I have experienced loneliness and social isolation, but the depth of peace and connection I've felt in my bones and with the Earth has been more than worth it.

Some years ago I did a ceremonial dance on Tiwa country in view of their Place of Emergence (Great Sand Dunes National Park in Colorado).[3] Deserts strip away all that isn't necessary and are powerful places to do ceremony. It was the height of summer, easily 40°C/100°F. The ceremony began with a sweat lodge, and then we dancers entered a dry fast, which means no food or water while we're in ceremony for the next few days. The idea is that we are spiritually supported to purify ourselves from all the lack-based energies we are carrying. I have danced in a few such ceremonies and rarely if ever felt physical hunger or thirst, though I have had a lot of stuff come up to let go of and process. At the centre of the dance arbour was a small, resilient tree that must've been quite old to have survived so long in the desert. By day I alternately danced to sacred drumming and rested, and by night I slept in a tent at the dance arbour. Each morning at sunrise we gathered to face east and chanted prayers of thanks as Grandmother Moon set and Grandfather Sun rose.

At one point while dancing, I fell to my knees at the tree in the centre of the arbour because I felt how deeply the tree, the land and the people loved me. I felt for the first time profoundly wanted and held by Mother Earth. I hadn't realised how disconnected from my inherent worthiness I had been, and I wept in gratitude for this reminder and then I wept with grief for all the lack I had been living with. When I left the desert I felt raw and shaky, yet stronger in my body than I could remember. I had a new lens on life, and everywhere I went I saw people who weren't aware of their inherent worth and how much we are all wanted and loved by Mother Earth.

It helped me see the depth of Wetiko (week 9) in the world, and to find my way to connecting with other people who are also consciously aware of this challenge. Despite all of the healing I experienced in the moment, I knew it would take time and effort to integrate that sense of worthiness into my daily life. It's been an important journey, and one that has cost me many relationships and cemented my role as a social outlier. Just like I wept at the tree with grief, I have wept since the ceremony for many endings. And just like I wept with gratitude for the knowing of my inherent worth and how much the Earth loves and wants me here, I have been filled up since the ceremony by enriching relationships and healing experiences.

We initially considered ceremony in week 5, and though we do them and feel their power, we may still feel insecure and uncertain, even if we know that they help us connect with our ancestors and feel more embodied. Potawatomi scientist Dr Kimmerer wrote that many of her ceremonies felt second-hand because she 'spoke in the language of exiles' and didn't know the true ceremonies or their names: 'It may have been a secondhand ceremony, but even through my confusion I recognized that the earth drank it up as if it were right. The land knows you, even when you are lost . . . [W]hat else can you offer the earth, which has everything . . . but something of yourself?'[4]

The Anishinaabe word *Miskâsowin* is described as going to the centre of yourself to find your own belonging. Sometimes we do this through ceremony, exemplified by my story of feeling belonging in the desert. Another way is through seeking out and honouring stories that 'remind us of who we are and of our belonging'[5] (week 31). And a third way is by discerning different aspects of our spiritual self to better understand our place in the universe. One way this may be explained is to: '[P]icture yourself as having a spirit with four parts . . . Your big spirit originates . . . in sky camp, while your ancestral spirit belongs to a specific place . . . Your shadow spirit is made of all your thoughts, attachments, ego and intent, while your living spirit is the energy that gives your body vitality.'[6]

If this perspective resonates with you, you can see why connecting with your ancestral spirit would help you feel grounded and centred in your body on Mother Earth. I have heard a number of Indigenous people who move to their traditional lands describe experiencing a profound quieting of the mind and a deep peace there. I have also heard multicultural people with many ancestral lineages describe moving to a place and realising they were 'in the centre of their story' or feeling like it was 'exactly where they were meant to be' and describing how their lives were flowing much better than they had before, and how much more centred they were feeling.

EXERCISE

Reflect on when, where and with whom you experience belonging across all areas of the medicine wheel (mental, emotional, spiritual, physical). What does it feel like? How does your mind show up? What happens in your body? What is the state of being of your spirit?

Now consider Ngurra-kurlu, the home within (week 43) that includes Family, Law, Land, Language and Ceremony. Which of those do you feel strong in? What do you need to deepen your sense of belonging in your inner and outer worlds? Reflect on a step you might take by asking your wise inner self, trusted people in your life and/or ancestors.

Holiness

WEEK BEGINNING: _____

SEASON: _____

The etymology of the world 'holy' is 'healthy' and 'whole'. 'Holy', 'sacred', 'blessed' and 'divine' all refer to something valuable that is treated with reverence and respect.

EXERCISE

What does the phrase 'holy land' bring into your mind?

For many of us the phrase 'holy land' is biblical and we think of Israel. Though I agree that the land we call Israel is holy, I encourage you to reclaim, decolonise and expand your association of this phrase. To elevate one particular place as holy is to denote others as less holy or even unholy. This is a dangerous thing to do if it becomes existential. Considering that our bodies are connected with Mother Earth, if only one place is holy land, then billions of us are in exile not feeling whole, missing the opportunity to honour sacred land beneath our feet and feel grounded or centred where we are.

If I want my whole being, and certainly my whole physical body, to be treated with reverence and respect, then I want to reciprocally treat Mother Earth and the resources she shares with us with reverence and respect as well. It may seem tough to do that in a society where so much is taken for granted. Sometimes we may remember holiness by bearing witness to acts of desecration. For example, when I buy something I often look at where it was made, consider which resources went into it and feel into the spirit it embodies. This process tends to bring up pain, even when I buy 'eco' products that feel a bit better than their corporate counterparts. When I get a new phone, I reflect on the mined and manmade materials that went into it, how many lands they came from, and the human labour that went into mining, building, packaging and transporting it that led to the phone being a tool for me to use.

Another way to treat the Earth's resources as holy is to use them for as long as possible – even when outdated or glitchy (like right now, my phone's home button has stopped working but I found a workaround). I keep it clean – in terms of internal memory and storage and external screen and case – and even smudge it now and then. I also take time to sit in awe about the fact that such a tool has even been created and how grateful I am to be able to do so many things, including communicate with loved ones around the world, navigate, take photos, watch videos and listen to music and keep organised with a calendar and alarm clock. If the company that made this phone had a vision of planned obsolescence, I don't have to share that. Maybe eating organic is better, or maybe eating GMO that was grown, harvested and cooked with reverence is better.

Part of what may make us feel less than holy is a version of a Judeo-Christian teaching that we are 'sinful' by nature, explained as all humans being punished and shameful due to Adam and Eve eating an apple (or was it a fig?[1]). Yet the Hebrew word *chait*, which is commonly translated into English as 'sin', is 'more accurately translated simply as "error" or "mistake"'.[2] From this perspective, the word 'sin' is meant to help us understand our nature as humans: that we are powerful and also tend to make mistakes, not that we are exiled, unworthy, or that our sacred Mother Earth doesn't innately and fully love and support us.

Celtic Australian scientist Dr Glenys Livingstone shares her experience with this teaching of 'sin' and how disembodied it led her to feel, saying: 'I had no sense of relationship with my earthly and cosmic habitat. [The Earth] was a big dead ball of dirt . . . from which we would be saved by "God" eventually . . . the supernatural Christian drama of God and Jesus was completely unrelated to place. It was a particularly cerebral religion.'[3]

That is not everyone's experience with Christianity or other Abrahamic religions, but it was hers, it was also mine, and it may be yours.

Even if this resonates with you just a little, chances are you would benefit from integrating a bit more holiness into your life. You may want to start with the concept of a 'holyday' or a 'holiday'. In most Western countries, these days align with significant events for Christians and days designated as important to the story of a nation state. If those days feel holy to you, that's wonderful. And if they don't feel especially important, that's okay. There can be an everyday baseline of holiness in life as well as extra-special days, just like all land can be holy and still contain specific sacred sites. For example, I do ceremony for the winter solstice instead of Christmas, though I enjoy the collective feeling of so many people resting and rejoicing on 25 December. I invite you to try the thought exercise on the next page.

EXERCISE

Imagine what life would look and feel like if:

⊙ every land you walked upon was treated as holy land

⊙ each human body you came into contact with
including your own was treated as holy

⊙ all of creation was treated as holy, so that every animal and plant you ate,
every mineral mined and every material built with was treated as holy

⊙ every action you took was a holy ritual

⊙ each day was holy

⊙ each season and all forms of weather were holy, even climate change

⊙ your entire life was a ceremony filled with holy rituals.

Reflect on how you currently carry and embody holiness in your life across all areas of the medicine wheel. What, if anything, could practically support you to more fully integrate this vision and these feelings into your everyday life?

WEEK

47

Initiation

WEEK BEGINNING: _____

SEASON: _____

Initiations are rites of passage ceremonies marking existential life transitions. An important one across Indigenous and Western cultures is the transition from spiritual child into spiritual adult. Abagusii scientist Mircea Eliade describes it thus: 'Initiation introduces the candidate into the human community and . . . the world of spiritual and cultural values . . . [including:] behavior patterns . . . techniques, and . . . institutions of adults . . . sacred myths and traditions of the tribe . . . gods . . . [and] mystical relations between the tribe and the Supernatural Beings . . . established at the beginning of Time.'[1]

Initiations intentionally lead us through Earth's cycle from life into death then rebirth with a new identity through a purposefully traumatic process (week 11). As one Western psychologist explains: 'The initiate, by virtue of encountering ritual trauma, was prepared to meet real-life trauma on terms that were integrative to the tribe's social system and spiritual beliefs. Rather than encounter trauma as senseless and random . . . the initiate could meet trauma as an opportunity for meaningful participation with the greater spiritual powers.'[2]

Initiations may be seen as having three distinct phases: separation (from daily reality), ordeal (trauma) and return (rebirth and resolution).[3] The separation phase tends to include seclusion from family and time in the wilderness to take us out of everyday familiarity into unknown energies and into encounters with the elements, spirits and our non-human kin. In many Indigenous cultural traditions, men are put through painful initiation ordeals whereas women's initiation is considered to be biologically built into the sacred ordeals of pregnancy and childbirth.[4] In some cultures, though, women are put through ordeals as well.[5] Spiritual initiations are painful because we tend to value what we earn through hard work, and we learn best through lived experiences.

Interestingly, a South Saami creation story teaches that this entire world is the result of our previously taking the Earth's bounty for granted and needing strong reminders of the value of her resources.[6] This is similar to what I was told by some Mayan people in 2012 when the Western media was reporting that the Mayan calendar said the world was going to end. 'No,' they told me, 'our calendar says that in 2012 we are collectively moving out of spiritual childhood as a human species and into adolescence, and into a different calendar.' They said overall we will become consciously aware that Mother Earth requires reciprocity, that we cannot just take from her and that there are consequences for our use of the Earth's resources.

One example of an ordeal is the Sateré-Mawé tradition of adolescent boys enduring the pain of repeatedly putting their hand into a glove filled with bullet ants that inject toxins into them.[7] They are called bullet ants because the intensity of the poison they inject is meant to hurt as much as being shot. The boys are expected to endure this willingly, silently and stoically, which teaches them to be hunters who can handle the toughest aspects of their Amazonian jungle home and affirms values such as courage and strength. It also represents a loss of innocence by teaching that their environment can be dangerous, and even deadly, for after each session of placing a hand into the ant-ridden glove, boys are given medicine that makes them purge. Keeping the ant toxins in their body can have very impactful lifelong effects, such as loss of sanity. The myth is that the ants originate from the vagina of an underworld snake woman – an embodiment of the dark side of the sacred feminine and the Earth Herself.[8]

Initiations thus teach cultural myths and values, and ordeals without sacred spiritual stories attached to them, are merely meaningless violence, reinforcing nihilism and lacking re-integration and fulfilment of a new identity along with its social responsibilities. In the example above, boys who make it through the initiation are allowed to hunt and marry, which completes their rebirth as adult men in the community. Many of us grew up in cultures with rites of passage that included separation and ordeal phases but lacked full return phases to reintegrate us into a healthy new identity. We may feel called to question our cosmology (week 10) and find a way to rebirth ourselves without collective ceremony or recognition of our hard work.

EXERCISE

What partial or full initiations have you been through?
Were they facilitated by other people or simply lived experience?
If it was a full initiation, how do you celebrate your new identity?
If it was a partial initiation, work with your ancestors and reflect on how
you may complete it to feel whole and celebrate your new identity.

WEEK

48

Magic

WEEK BEGINNING: _____

SEASON: _____

W hen I use the word 'magic' I am referring broadly to spiritual and supernatural actions, interactions and interventions. It is challenging to write about this because English terminology is tricky, and there is so much diversity among Indigenous cultures. For example, the word 'shaman' is often used to describe a medicine person, but it is a term appropriated from Siberian peoples. And the word 'magic' could be interchanged with 'sorcery', 'witchcraft', 'mystic' or even 'manifestation' in some people's minds.

The way magic is generally used in Indigenous science is to 'coax nature to do its job, not to replace it'.[1] As an example, when building a house traditional cultures still did their best to practically engineer sturdy structures, but also used magic to seek protection through unusual weather events. Keep in mind what is magic is relative – in many cultures technology like mobile phones or airplanes are considered magic.[2] Also keep in mind that certain terminology may be best decolonised, such as 'black' or 'dark' magic being bad – this actually has a racist history.[3]

There are many different magic skills, gifts and social roles, and becoming more aware of yours supports you to live in a way that better aligns with your culture, core values and calling. The way I think about being a medicine person, or a 'shaman', is like being a general practitioner doctor – you need a variety of skills and awareness of your limits so you know when to refer someone to a specialist. Magic skills and gifts may include (but are not limited to):

⊙ plant medicine, such as herbalism, creating potions and salves, facilitating psychedelic plant ceremonies and plant communication (like dietas)

⊙ psychic healing, such as visualisations, divination (seeing what happened already), oracle work (seeing what will happen), psychic surgery (just like it sounds: a non-physical 'surgery' to heal wounds), spells or affirmations and prayers for manifesting or sorcery (there are many types of sorcery, which may be used destructively and/or constructively)

⊙ oracle work and divination done physically, such as reading tea leaves or using a divining rod to find ley lines in the land, or ceremonially sacrificing an animal to determine whether someone has cursed someone else

- law work, such as upholding cultural law and directing others how to, revival of cultural laws (noting that laws in Indigenous science derive from the land and are embodied in cultural lore; they are not changeable like Western law)
- physical healing, such as laying of the hands, touch healing systems (like the Hawai'ian Ho'olomilomi massage),[4] body movement and breath healing systems (like yoga), physical and energy healing systems (like acupuncture within traditional Chinese medicine) and dance (such as imitating animals or ecstatic dance)
- energy healing such as moving energy through the body, removing energetic blockages and channelling or facilitating celestial beings, ancestors and/or other spirits to heal someone
- symbolic healing, such as the use of words or letters through prayers, sorcery or spells or affirmations, runes and ancient symbols and sacred geometry
- spirit or ancestor communication, such as channelling, possession and altar work
- release work, such as extractions, exorcisms, curse removal and healing traumas
- story healing, such as facilitating talking circles or empathic dialogues, storytelling, passing on cultural myths and storytelling through other mediums such as visual art, dance, song or ceremony
- ceremony work, such as supporting an individual's vision quest or facilitating an entire community's trance dance, initiations and psychopomp work (supporting souls on their afterlife 'crossing-over' journey)
- animal work, such as physical, psychic and/or spiritual communication, shapeshifting, working with a familiar or guide and kinship care
- creating magical tools, such as carving crystals, rocks or wood into shapes such as wands, animals or totem poles, art healing (like Diné /Navajo sand painting), making jewellery or clothing imbued with sorcery or prayers and making objects or effigies to be used in sorcery (like 'voodoo dolls')
- sound healing, such as with singing or crystal bowls, chanting, didgeridoos, drumming and singing medicine songs
- sub- and unconscious work, such as dream work, astral travel, spirit flight, soul retrieval, or even walking the land to revive lost language and other Indigenous knowledge.

If you have not heard of some of these, don't worry. Trust your intuition and guidance about what to learn and develop and how deep to go.

EXERCISE

First, considering the list above, make note of what
you resonate with. Which do you feel competent in?
Which do you wish to learn or develop more?

*Second, considering what your gifts and skills are, ask yourself what role you would
likely have in your culture(s). You may need to ask Elders or do some research
about traditional roles to better understand what roles were in your culture(s).*

Third, reflect on how to honour your role, gifts and skills best in your life today.

*(For example, someone skilled at manifestation who has a vivid imagination
and some trauma healing skills may be a sorcerer, magician or wizard in their
traditional culture. That person may find fulfilment through working as a spiritual
healer. And someone who is passionate about upholding laws and ensuring their
relationships are just and morally righteous may be a traditional law person
who finds alignment in modern life by working as a mediator or advocate.)*

Embodiment

WEEK BEGINNING: _____

SEASON: _____

Being authentic, centred and grounded means having awareness of our core values and doing our best to enliven them through our life choices and forms of expression. Embodiment is a recognition of the universality of our connection with all of creation as well as our individuality of lived experience. It's important not to confuse lived experience knowledge with intellectual understanding or awareness, often referred to as 'knowledge' in Western science. We all have intellectual understanding and awareness about life experiences we haven't had; for example, we may say that −10°C is cold, but unless we've felt it, we don't have an embodied knowing of how cold that is.

There is so much power in lived experience that from an Indigenous science perspective, it is the only way we can 'know' something. People with a lot Western theoretical or book 'knowledge' are often seen as arrogant, or even dangerous. If we've learned some 'evidence-based' ways to prevent obesity, we will still have a limited ability to empathise with people who have experienced it themselves or witnessed it through an intimate relationship.

Knowing our standing, or positionality, makes a huge difference in how well we embody our values and medicine. Our standing refers to our placement – sociopolitically, culturally, physically, emotionally, mentally and spiritually. I've included sociopolitically and culturally because we live in two worlds as Indigenous scientists and need to be aware of our Western political placement as well as Indigenous cultural placement.

As an Indigenous scientist living far from ancestral lands, from a sociopolitical perspective I am a settler[1] doing my best to be a political ally[2] of Aboriginal peoples of Australia. I can't experience what's embodied through their cultural lineages and relationships; they carry a power of intergenerational knowledge that, if shared with me, supports me to build my own relationships with their ancestors and the land where I live. Gitksan scientist Dr Cindy Blackstock explains Indigenous scientific trust in long-tested ancestral wisdom and our collective responsibility for carrying and passing on Indigenous knowledge: 'Because knowledge needs to echo across lifetimes and generations, multidimensional standards of rigor are needed to ensure knowledge is understood within the four dimensions of learning: spiritual, emotional, physical and cognitive and that each teaching is situated within an interconnected knowledge web.'[3]

It's natural to speak about things we haven't experienced at times, but it's wise to do so with humility in recognition of our standing within that interconnected web of life. For without lived experience (which includes knowledge embedded in our bodies through ancestral inheritance), to some extent we are guessing and imagining.

Embodied methods for sharing traditional knowledge have helped ensure its efficacy and accuracy over time and prevented the impact of such human limitations from diluting or distorting it. As Western science researcher Dr Lynne Kelly explains, 'At every level of initiation into knowledge there were memory aids . . . from hand-held objects to art on bark or rocks, to the landscape itself',[4] in addition to songs and stories that were easy to remember yet cleverly layered with knowledge.[5] This is why changing landscapes and moving Indigenous peoples can be severely disorienting and detrimental to cultural integrity.

EXERCISE

Reflect on embodied memory aids you have – such as objects in your house, photos, places you go, music and so on. Which ones bring you joy? Which ones feel like clutter that could be let go? Are there any that trigger you into trauma or other difficult emotion? If so, do you wish to let them go or ceremonially cleanse them?

It's helpful to consider that our bodies themselves 'speak' stories, with our bones showing how nourished we are, our body's ergonomic strain and even our toxin exposure.[6] Our bodies also arouse stories in others. Shona scientist Dr Virginia Mapedzahama says when she walks into a room she experiences predetermined sociopolitical space simply because of her Black body,[7] whereas Yuin scientist Shannon Field describes awareness of her sociopolitical privilege since she can pass as White though she is a Blak Aboriginal woman.[8]

To further complicate things, many of us have lived experiences that aren't fully processed. For example, if someone believes that lying makes them a 'bad person', they may subconsciously trick themselves and others into believing an altered story that omits a 'bad' thing they did. An acute listener will likely experience cognitive dissonance, a sense that the storyteller's heart and head were in conflict. This highlights the importance of using discernment (week 35) with shared knowledge, even when it is embodied.

EXERCISE

Reflect on what spaces around you embody,
such as a school, park or prison.

Reflect on what social structures embody, such as a performer on stage above an audience or a judge sitting higher than the jury, victim, lawyers or the accused.

Reflect on your life and what you embody and what you intentionally wish to.

WEEK

50

Law and justice

WEEK BEGINNING: _____

SEASON: _____

When you see 'law' and 'justice' you likely think of judges and courtrooms. This Western version is pervasive around the world, though it is but one manifestation of a collective cultural understanding of justice. Let's decolonise our minds.

First, let's consider the source of law. In Indigenous science law comes from the Earth, which is why some Indigenous people today are literally walking their traditional lands to revive language, lore and law. Lore refers to stories (week 32) that teach law, and language, lore and law are intertwined. For example, in Aboriginal Australian Indigenous languages there is no word that translates the concept of 'safety' from English; culturally, the concept of protection is the best translation, which is used to describe everyone's responsibilities for taking care of each other, not an idea of a 'right' that people are entitled to have protected by institutions such as the police.[1]

The Western concept of 'natural law' is based on 'God, nature, and reason' and is considered to be inherent, which makes it the basis of all 'rights'.[2] There is also the concept of 'positive law', which refers to how we humans ground natural law in a civilised society, such as through legislation. These concepts are of course based on a Western cosmological understanding of creation, nature and human nature. Indigenous cosmologies have different understandings of creation, nature and the primacy of reason in a society, and so naturally laws and justice differ as well.

For example, an Indigenous science perspective of human nature is that we are humble caretakers interconnected with the place where we live and all other beings there. If we move we have to seek permission from the beings living in that place, human and non-human, in order to live there at all, and learn how to do so in the right way. This is a very different view to colonisation, which was based on ideas of sovereignty being claimable and some people and non-human kin being of less worth than others. It is also a very different view to Christianisation, which was based on the idea that a specific spiritual tradition was the only legitimate path to follow.

The reason the Earth is where law and culture come from is because that is where our lives are sustained, so that is where we have reciprocal responsibilities as members of an ecosystem.[3] Our ecosystem's health is intimately connected with and reflective of human health. As one Malanbarra and Dulabed Yidinji scientist explained to a Western scientist: 'The river is us! We protect it more and want to protect it more, and we want to make sure that whoever uses this river uses it properly . . . come down and stop the damaging of places, because we have sites on the river, we have burials, men's and women's places.'[4]

There are a few examples of non-humans such as rivers and non-human animals being extended rights under Western law so that they become 'legal persons'. We may notice how human centric the phrase 'legal person' is and how strange it sounds describing a river. We may wonder whether referring to a non-human as an 'it' is dehumanising, and we may feel frustrated that there is no non-human-centric word to describe the concept of stripping a being of dignity and life, like 'de-life-ifying'. This is another example of language, law and lore being intertwined; in this case, the story is about humans being at the centre of creation, rather than actors within an ecosystem.

Indigenous law is revealed through Indigenous science data, including natural embodied experiences in everyday life as well as revelations, dreams, visions, ceremonies and other connections with 'supernatural' aspects of being. Laws are embodied and passed on in daily rituals and sacred ceremonies, embedded into language, and reflected in the sky and the land. For example, the Tiwa of North America believe that humans exist in order to reconcile polarities and that our walk of life is a metaphor for this process, so in their language the word *nah-meh-nay* refers to land, which means the 'self that purifies'.[5] Laws are changed by consensus based on Indigenous processes of governance (week 41), which means it may take longer for them to change than in a majority rule system, but when they do it is due to sustainable social change.

Most Indigenous peoples use oral traditions to preserve a sense of sameness; when oral teachings are passed from Elders to the younger generation, there is no document open to interpretation. There is an understanding that verbal repetition, not writing, keeps stories and teachings pure. Laws may be traditionally upheld in Indigenous cultures by people with cultural authority referred to as 'lawmen'. They help mediate conflicts as well as prevent and atone for offending against other humans, non-human kin and supernatural beings. They may also be upheld by aggrieved community members, such as with ceremonial spearing (week 36).

'Justice' refers to how laws are administered so that we live in the 'right way'. Though there are different understandings of what living in the right way means in Western culture, and therefore what justice looks like practically, an Indigenous justice process must consider whether humans are capable of administering certain laws at all or if that is the role of the Creator.[6] Some Indigenous people say that when we stop acknowledging the natural forces greater than us, negative things happen to remind us of our place in the world as humans.[7]

EXERCISE

Consider language, lore and law. What frustrates you about English (like pronouns and binary gender identities)? When do you feel conflict with lore (like the myth of the American Dream) and law (like the age of being a legal adult)? How might you address one of these issues in your own life in an embodied way? What are some limits and struggles you feel when confronting ungrounded law, language and lore?

For example, to address ancestral land theft my partner and I have decided not to own land in Australia. This creates struggles for us now as renters, and different struggles in future if we wish to buy land and hold it in another form than personal ownership such as a legal trust with traditional custodians as trustees.

Integrity

WEEK BEGINNING: _____

SEASON: _____

W e first considered boundaries and integrity in week 21. I invite you now to revisit these topics using the medicine wheel exercise template from week 2.

EXERCISE

What does integrity mean to you now (spiritually, emotionally, physically and mentally? Fill in the medicine wheel template below.

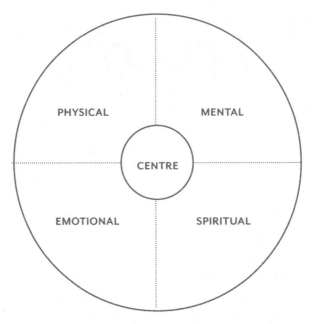

What's changed since you last considered integrity and boundaries (week 21) and this exercise (week 2)? What does this medicine wheel tell you about your identity?

Something I gained more clarity about through the course of writing this book is around my embodiment of trickster (week 24) in order to live in both Indigenous and Western cosmologies. I know through being confronted with life choices that I value truth so much I am willing to stake my livelihood, intimate relationships and even my life on it. But I can be truthful to a fault, such as when it's not important (like someone asking how I am when they really mean 'hello'), or when something can cause me harm and isn't worth fighting over (like telling a little protective lie to avoid being punished by a judgemental family member).

Of course, we each have to live with our choices, but by being honest with myself about where I'm using trickster energy, I feel more at peace about my integrity. I have to find ways to survive in the Western world just like everyone else who carries an Indigenous cosmology. I shop in a grocery store as well as grow and forage for food. I work in the gift economy as well as the transactional economy. My integrity, and my survival, rely on integrating Indigenous and Western ways in my daily life. The poem on the following page came to me a few years ago about this journey.

Land bridge

My heart is Indigenous
In sync with the seasons
My feet firmly grounded
In Mother Earth below me.
My spirit is Indigenous
Interconnected with all that is
Flaming with animist passion
For peaceful coexistence.
My mind is Indigenous
Built upon a cosmology
Of communal integrity
Wholeness and ease.
My soul is Indigenous
Ravished with pain
In states of mankind's
Civilising war games.
My name is Indigenous
Given during a spiritual journey
Cloud Clearer, who helps release
Dis-eased thinking.
I challenge cultural exclusion
Indigenous and non-indigenous
Living between identities
I cry out for community.

I want you to know that if you are integrating Indigenous science into your life, whether people around you see or appreciate your effort, it matters and you are inherently valuable whatever your choices and struggles. On a spiritual level you are part of my, and the entire Earth's, sacred community, and I thank you for being your whole self.

EXERCISE

Reflect on what it means to you to integrate Indigenous and Western science in your life moving forward. Where does it flow? Where do you experience values conflicts and challenges to your integrity?

WEEK

52

Humour

WEEK BEGINNING: _____

SEASON: _____

A

mong the principles of Indigenous science shared in week 1 was keeping a lightness of heart and sense of humour. Sioux scientist Dr Vine Deloria Jr said humour is one of the best ways to understand a people and that 'laughter encompasses the limits of the soul'.[1] As Anishinaabe comedian Stephanie Pangowish explains: 'Our hearts are so big, and our spirits are so beautiful that that's how we've come to terms with things: by making it not as big — making it so that these situations that we're in aren't bigger than our hearts, you know? By making fun of it, it becomes smaller.'[2]

Among many Indigenous cultures, teasing has been traditionally used for social control, and people often use it to poke fun at themselves.[3] The character of Wile E. Coyote, whose scheming always backfires, is based on the coyote as trickster (week 24) archetype of native peoples of the American south-west. Remembering that we each play the trickster sometimes – we trick others and we get tricked – keeps us humble and creates opportunities for laughter to bring joy into tough situations.

Years ago I was working two jobs: one as an unpaid advocate for clergy sex abuse survivors, and another doing paid ad-hoc policy research for a large charity. I was burning the candle at both ends, and when a car knocked me off my bike while I was riding in a bike lane to the unpaid job, I knew something had to give. I had just been offered a permanent part-time role doing the policy research and knew it was wise to take that job, but my clergy abuse colleague was worried our activism would miss its moment if we lost momentum. So I took a chance on the passion project, and through a priest supporter I was gifted a small stipend with the promise of more to come. I dove in and it seemed to flow – we had journalists asking us for information, meetings with government officials and other allies, and even threatening letters from church lawyers. We worked into the night and laughed about our lack of resources and yet how scared the church officials had become of us. And then we laughed about how we had managed to laugh about something as heavy as clergy sex abuse.

It worked – within the year we had helped bring about the first inquiry into clergy sex abuse in Australia. And it didn't work – as I found myself without the promised financial support for a visa sponsorship to remain in

Australia. This wasn't the first time I had poured my heart into something without taking good care of myself financially. And while passion projects still matter a lot to me, I learned the hard way not to turn down a gift of a solid part-time job in order to play Icarus. (If you don't know the story, it's a Greek myth in which a boy called Icarus had a father who made him wings of feather and wax to escape imprisonment, but warned him not to fly too high and close to the sun for the heat would melt the wax. Icarus did fly too close to the sun and plummeted into the sea, where an island named after him embedded his story into the land so that we could learn from it forevermore.)

Looking back, it seems quite ridiculous to turn down financial stability and interesting work with kind people that was only part time, so I could have still done the clergy sex-abuse activism part time as well. When the visa sponsorship didn't come through, I felt devastated to be leaving Australia abruptly after building so many relationships, and ashamed to have to move back into my parents' house in my early 30s due to my poor financial choices. It was many years before I proved to myself that I could make better financial choices and still engage in passion projects in a meaningful way. And though I'm still not the most pragmatic about money, I can laugh at my foolish younger self and know that I won't turn down such a gift again!

One of the paradoxes of life is how much more we learn and grow through trauma (week 11) and ordeal (week 47) than when things flow smoothly. How we handle ourselves through challenging experiences says a lot about our spirit. There is a lot of power in being able to make a joke when we are hurting, or make fun of the situation we got ourselves into when we are feeling ashamed. And there's power in quietly holding pain with compassion when it feels like there's too much sensitivity to make light of a situation. For example, I had a friend who struggled for years to get pregnant and eventually gave up. When I tried I got pregnant quite quickly, but being close to me was too painful for her. Though humour is important medicine, it requires right timing to land. I encourage you to now take some time to laugh at yourself in a way that you feel ready to through the following exercise.

EXERCISE

Reflect on a time you played the fool in your past. Write or tell that story to someone and enjoy a good laugh at your own expense. How does it feel?

Now reflect on something you feel some heavy emotion around, such as shame. Ask yourself, and perhaps also a loved one or your ancestors, for a way to bring more lightness into that space. What do you need to be able to laugh about it just a little?

This week wouldn't be complete without at least sharing one joke, so here we go. Two whales are swimming and spot a ship. One says, 'The guys on that ship killed my father! We have to get revenge.' The other asks what they should do, and the first replies, 'We will swim under the ship and use our tails to flip it over.' They do so, but the first whale is still not satisfied. 'They're not hurting,' he says, 'they're just bobbing in the water. In order to really get back at them we have to kill them like they killed my father. Let's eat them now!' The second whale, however, is not pleased with this new request. 'Whoa, whoa, whoa!' he says. 'I agreed to your blow job, I did not agree to swallow your seamen!'

I hope that gave you a giggle. If you can't think of a good joke sometime when you're feeling down and want an easy pick me up, try the following exercise and you may be amazed by how easily you can shift your spirit into lighter-heartedness.

EXERCISE

Start forcing yourself to laugh, being silly about it if you like, and see how little time it takes for it to turn into real laughter. (Keep this in mind next time you or a loved one is in need of a pick-me-up moment.)

Closing

I hope you have enjoyed this medicine wheel year, and that you have picked up tools and insights along the way in service of yourself, your ancestors and all of creation. If you have received something of value from this book, please engage in reciprocity by living, giving and sharing the learnings.

There are many layers to the topics in this book, so you may wish to revisit some chapters and exercises in years to come. If you want to share your story about this journey or embark on further journeys with related teachings, you may connect with me through the Earth Ethos website, blog and social media. You may also enjoy reading some of the books cited here such as Robin Wall Kimmerer's *Braiding Sweetgrass*, Tyson Yunkaporta's *Sand Talk* or Svieby and Skuthorpe's *Treading Lightly*.

May your life be an ever-deepening journey of re-membering your innate worth and cosmological indigeneity so that we all live with more dignity and integrity in honour of ourselves, our ancestors and all of creation.

Appendix

An **equinox** occurs when *day and night are equal in length*. The beginning of astronomical spring is marked by a vernal equinox, and the beginning of autumn is marked by an autumnal equinox. I started writing this book just before the spring equinox. A **solstice** occurs when the sun is at its highest or lowest point in the sky and marks the *longest and shortest days of the year*. The beginning of astronomical summer is signalled by the summer solstice, and the beginning of winter is signalled by the winter solstice. A quarter or cross-quarter day signifies the midpoint or peak of an astronomical season.

Keep in mind that seasons differ in the northern and southern hemispheres and that Celtic names are often used for quarter and cross-quarter days.

EQUINOX/SOLSTICE	SOUTHERN HEMISPHERE	NORTHERN HEMISPHERE
Autumn equinox	Third week of March	Third week of September
Winter solstice	Third week of June	Third week of December
Spring equinox	Third week of September	Third week of March
Summer solstice	Third week of December	Third week of June

QUARTER AND CROSS-QUARTER DAYS	SOUTHERN HEMISPHERE	NORTHERN HEMISPHERE
Lady Day/Ostara	Between 21–24 September	Around 21–22 March
Midsummer Day/Litha	Around 21 December	Around 21 June
Michaelmas/Mabon	Around 21–22 March	Between 21–24 September
Midwinter/Yule	Around 21–22 June	Around 21 December
Candlemas/Imbolc	1 August	1 February
May Day/Beltane	1 November	1 May
Lammas/Lughnasadh	1 February	Around 1 August
Halloween/Samhain	1 May	31 October

Endnotes

WEEK 1

1. Brian McNeill and Jose M. Cervantes (eds) (2008), *Latina/o Healing Practices: Mestizo and Indigenous Perspectives*, Routledge, New York.
2. Apela Colorado and Kit Cooley, 'Remembering Who We Are: Recovering Indigenous Mind', Worldwide Indigenous Science Network, www.wisn.org, 31 August 2013, Appendix A: Nine Distinctions of Indigenous Science.

WEEK 2

1. Joseph Rael, *Ceremonies of the Living Spirit*, Council Oak Books, Oklahoma, 1998, p. 35.
2. Wikipedia, 'Medicine wheel (symbol)', https://en.wikipedia.org/wiki/Medicine_wheel_(symbol)#/media/File:Medicine_Wheel.png.
3. Wikipedia, 'Vitruvian Man', https://en.wikipedia.org/wiki/Vitruvian_Man.

WEEK 3

1. See for example Sean Hoen, HealthCentral, Adrenal Fatigue: Is it Real?', https://www.endocrineweb.com/conditions/adrenal-disorders/adrenal-fatigue.
2. https://en.wikipedia.org/wiki/Tree_of_life.
3. See for example Wally Brown, YouTube, Are There Invisible Senses?, https://www.youtube.com/watch?v=YYFLOHt1nxk
4. Western science is honouring this recently through, for example, 1,000 Days, 'The 1,000 days from pregnancy to age two offer a crucial window of opportunity to create brighter, healthier futures', https://thousanddays.org/why-1000-days/.

WEEK 4

1. See for example National Library of Medicine, 'Earthing: Health Implications of Reconnecting the Human Body to the Earth's Surface Electrons', https://www.ncbi.nlm.nih.gov/pmc/articles/PMC3265077/ and articles cited in SOTT, 'Studies show what happens to the human body when we walk barefoot', https://www.sott.net/article/360215-Studies-show-what-happens-to-the-human-body-when-we-walk-barefoot.
2. Cortisol Matters, 'What is cortisol?', https://www.cortisolmatters.com/patient/what-is-cortisol.

WEEK 5

1. Polly Walker, 'Indigenous Ceremonial Peacemaking: The Restoration of Balance and Harmony', in *Handbook of Research on Promoting Peace Through Practice, Academia, and the Arts*, IGI Global, 2019, pp. 299–319.
2. Rael, *Ceremonies of the Living Spirit*.

WEEK 6

1. Thanks to Dakota Earth Cloud Walker for influencing my thinking; for example, Dakota Earth Cloud, YouTube, 'The Three Veins of Ancestors', https://www.youtube.com/watch?v=ubTuI5DFjL8.

WEEK 7

1. Please visit the Earth Ethos YouTube channel at https://www.youtube.com/channel/UCDodlpyH7PrpHhh9jSiZsIA.

WEEK 8

1. Polly Walker, 'Indigenous Ceremonial Peacemaking: The Restoration of Balance and Harmony', pp. 299–319.
2. Rupert Ross, *Returning to the Teachings: Exploring Aboriginal Justice*, Penguin Books, Toronto, Canada, 2006.
3. Karl-Erik Sveiby and Tex Skuthorpe, *Treading Lightly: The hidden wisdom of the world's oldest people*, Allen & Unwin, Sydney, 2006.

WEEK 9

1. Robin Wall Kimmerer, *Braiding Sweetgrass: Indigenous Wisdom, Scientific Knowledge, and the Teachings of Plants*, Milkweed Editions, Minneapolis, 2015, p. 307.
2. Tyson Yunkaporta, *Sand Talk: How Indigenous Thinking Can Save the World*, Text Publishing, 2019, p. 25.
3. Visit Australian Indigenous Astronomy, 'Yidumduma: A True Aboriginal Astronomer', http://aboriginalastronomy.blogspot.com/2011_07_01_archive.html for a great image of a dark emu constellation.
4. Leah Tonino, 'Robin Wall Kimmerer On Scientific And Native American Views Of The Natural World', *The Sun* magazine, April 2016.
5. Nicole M. Monteiro and Diana J. Wall, 'African Dance as Healing Modality Throughout the Diaspora: The Use of Ritual and Movement to Work Through Trauma, *Journal of Pan African Studies*, 4(6), 234–52, 2011.
6. Sudhir Kakar, *Shamans, Mystics, and Doctors: A Psychological Inquiry into India and Its Healing Traditions*, University of Chicago Press, Chicago, 1982.
7. Paul Levy, 'Dispelling Wetiko: Breaking the Curse of Evil', *Quest*, 102.4 (fall), 146–51.
8. McNeill and Cervantes, *Latina/o Healing Practices.*
9. Peter Wohlleben, *The Hidden Life of Trees: What They Feel, How They Communicate – Discoveries from a Secret World*, Greystone Books, Vancouver, 2016.
10. The figure is based on Steffen Lehmann, 'Reconnecting with nature: Developing urban spaces in the age of climate change', Emerald Open Research, 2019, https://emeraldopenresearch.com/articles/1-2.

WEEK 10

1. A great collection of creation myths can be found in David A. Leeming, *Creation myths of the world: An Encyclopedia*, 2nd ed., vol. 1, ABC-CLIO, Santa Barbara, 2009.
2. See for example Joseph Rael, *being & vibration: entering the new world*, Millichap Books, Tulsa, 2015.
3. David Dean, White Awake, 'Roots Deeper than Whiteness', https://whiteawake.org/2018/10/27/roots-deeper-than-whiteness/.

WEEK 11

1. See for example Judith Herman, *Trauma and Recovery: The Aftermath of Violence – From Domestic Abuse to Political Terror*, Basic Books, New York, 1992.
2. See for example Laurence J. Kirmayer, Robert Lemelson and Mark Barad (eds.), *Understanding Trauma: Integrating Biological, Clinical, and Cultural Perspectives*, Cambridge University Press, Cambridge, 2007, pp. 118–41.
3. Wikipedia, 'Eye movement desensitization and reprocessing', https://en.wikipedia.org/wiki/Eye_movement_desensitization_and_reprocessing.
4. Monteiro and Wall, 'African dance as healing modality throughout the diaspora'.
5. See for example David Kopacz and Joseph Rael, *Walking the Medicine Wheel: Healing Trauma & PTSD*, Millchap Books, Oklahoma, 2016.
6. See for example McNeill and Cervantes, *Latina/o Healing Practices.*
7. Sandra Nuñez, 'Brazil's Ultimate Healing Resource: The Power of Spirit' in Cervantes and McNeill, *Latina/o healing practices*, pp. 139–74.
8. See for example Roberta Culbertson, 'Embodied Memory, Transcendence, and Telling: Recounting Trauma, Re-Establishing the Self', *New Literary History*, 26(1), 169–95, 1995.
9. Earth Ethos, YouTube, 'Drum Journey Meditation', https://www.youtube.com/watch?v=1Bk10CmcuqQ.

WEEK 12

1. Kakar, *Shamans, Mystics, and Doctors*, p. 105.
2. For more information see Wikipedia, 'Ayahuasca', https://en.wikipedia.org/wiki/Ayahuasca.
3. Earth Ethos, YouTube, 'Body Relaxation', https://www.youtube.com/watch?v=WBaP1YClNNA&feature=youtu.be.
4. See for example, *The Northern Review* Marie-Francoise Guédon, 'Sacred Smokes in Circumboreal Countries: An Ethnobotanical Exploration'22, 2000, 29–42.

WEEK 13

1. Rael, *being & vibration.*

WEEK 14

1. See for example Peter Dockrill, Science Alert, 'The "Placebo Effect" Is Getting Even Stronger With Time, Study Finds', https://www.sciencealert.com/the-placebo-effect-is-somehow-getting-even-better-at-fooling-patients-study-finds.
2. A name I made up!

WEEK 15

1. Christina Pratt, Why Shamanism Now? (podcast), 'The Power of Faith', https://whyshamanismnow.com/2016/08/the-power-of-faith-2/.
2. Brianna Wiest, Thought Catalogue, 'This Year, Let Go Of The People Who Aren't Ready To Love You', https://thoughtcatalog.com/brianna-wiest/2023/01/next-year-let-go-of-the-people-who-arent-ready-to-love-you/.

WEEK 16

1. California State University, 'Chief Seattle's Letter to All', http://www.csun.edu/~vcpsy00h/seattle.htm.
2. Paul Valent, paulvalent.com, 'Survival Strategies Table', http://www.paulvalent.com/traumatic-stress-framework/survival-strategies-table/.

WEEK 17

1. See for example Anna Papadakis, Opening to Life, 'The Spiritual and Aboriginal Significance of The Placenta', https://www.openingtolife.com.au/the-spiritual-and-aboriginal-significance-of-the-placenta/.
2. Minmia (Maureen Smith), *Under the Quandong Tree*, Quandong Dreaming Publishing, Mogo, New South Wales, 2007.
3. Jodi Selander, Placenta Benefits.info, 'Culture: Cultural Beliefs Honor Placenta', https://placentabenefits.info/cultural-beliefs-honor-placenta/.
4. Placenta Remedies Network, 'Placenta History', https://placentaremediesnetwork.org/placenta-history/.
5. Essence Williams, Healthy Mom & Baby, 'Placenta Wisdom, Rituals and Traditions', https://www.health4mom.org/placenta-wisdom-rituals-and-traditions/#:~:text=Placentas%20Around%20the%20World&text=The%20Balinese%20wrap%20the%20placenta,or%20her%20homeland%20and%20ancestors.
6. Placenta Remedies Network, 'Placenta History'.
7. Ibid.
8. Selander, Placenta Benefits.info, 'Culture'.
9. Placenta Remedies Network, 'Placenta History'.
10. Selander, Placenta Benefits.info, 'Culture'.
11. Minmia, *Under the Quandong Tree*.
12. Ibid, p. 73.
13. Ibid, p. 75.

WEEK 18

1. See for example Justin Nobel, Digital Dying, 'In Asia, lying in coffins helps you live longer', https://www.funeralwise.com/digital-dying/in-asia-lying-in-coffins-helps-you-live-longer/.
2. See for example Natasha Geiling, *Smithsonian Magazine*, 'Festivals of the Dead Around the World', https://www.smithsonianmag.com/travel/festivals-dead-around-world-180953160/.
3. Ultra Deep Inner Game, YouTube, 'Guided Death Meditation', https://www.youtube.com/watch?v=2D-3w-5HUmQ.
4. Shantideva FPMT-Israel, YouTube, '8 "Stages of death" Meditation, https://www.youtube.com/watch?v=Azo95eWqw8k.

WEEK 19

1. Valerie, Earth Ethos, 'The Red Road', https://earthethos.net/2019/03/14/the-red-road2/.
2. Ross, *Returning to the Teaching3*.
3. Dean Jeffreys, YouTube, 'Anna Breytenbach communicates with Great White Shark', https://www.youtube.com/watch?v=HTdlMC6NZU4.

WEEK 22

1. Refer to Dr Gabor's website https://drgabormate.com/ and many talks freely available on YouTube.
2. For further information see Earth Ethos, YouTube, 'Ancestral healing dialogue', https://www.youtube.com/watch?v=ZD_SKctddsg.

WEEK 23

1. Nonie Sharp, *Stars of Tagai: The Torres Strait Islanders*, Aboriginal Studies Press, 2012.
2. Robin Wall Kimmerer, AllCreation.org, 'The "Honorable Harvest": Lessons From an Indigenous Tradition of Giving Thanks', http://www.allcreation.org/home/honorable.

WEEK 24

1. See for example William Reid and Robert Bringhurst, *The Raven Steals the Light*, Douglas & McIntyre, Canada, 1984.
2. For a list of many trickster figures see Wikipedia, 'Trickster', https://en.wikipedia.org/wiki/Trickster.
3. Brandi Morin, Al Jazeera, 'Indigenous people describe leaving towns to live off the land, learning lessons about survival from elders', https://www.aljazeera.com/indepth/features/indigenous-canada-turn-land-survive-coronavirus-200401073446077.html
4. For example Tanzanian president John Magufuli: Lynsey Chutel and Robbie Gramer, foreignpolicy.com, 'Tanzanian Leader Who Downplayed Pandemic Dies', https://foreignpolicy.com/2021/03/18/tanzanian-leader-mugufuli-coronavirus-dies-covid-africa/.

WEEK 25

1. See for example Wikipedia, 'Traditional Chinese medicine', https://en.wikipedia.org/wiki/Traditional_Chinese_medicine.
2. For a recipe see The Spruce Eats, 'Queimada (Galicia Fire Drink)', https://www.thespruceeats.com/queimada-recipe-fire-drink-of-galicia-3083122.

WEEK 27

1. See for example Mary Shutan, 'Should I use Psychedelics to Awaken?, https://maryshutan.com/should-i-use-psychedelics-to-awaken-the-seventh-eye-issue-7/.
2. Tina Fossella, 'Human Nature, Buddha Nature: An interview with John Welwood', Tricycle, The Buddhist Review, 20 (3), spring 2011.
3. Apela Colorado, *Woman Between the Worlds: A Call to Your Ancestral and Indigenous Wisdom*, Hay House, United Kingdom, 2021.
4. See for example Rael, *being & vibration*.
5. Arlin Cuncic, Very Well Mind, 'What is Cultural Appropriation?', https://www.verywellmind.com/what-is-cultural-appropriation-5070458.

WEEK 28

1. The word 'Sioux' includes Lakota and Dakota peoples and is how Dr Deloria referred to his culture.
2. Vine Deloria Jr and Daniel R. Wildcat, *Power and Place: Indian Education in America*, Fulcrum Publishing, Colorado, 2001.
3. Kent Nerburn and Jason Gardner (eds), *The Soul of an Indian: And other writings from Ohiyesa (Charles Alexander Eastman)*, New World Library, California, 2001.
4. Jarem Sawatsky, *The Ethic of Traditional Communities and the Spirit of Healing Justice: Studies from Hollow Water, the Iona Community, and Plum Village*, Jessica Kingsley Publishers, Philadelphia, 2009, p. 55 citing James Gilligan, *Preventing Violence (Prospects for Tomorrow)*, Thames & Hudson, New York, 2001.
5. See for example Steven Thibodeau and Gary Nixon, 'Transformation for native men with assaultive issues: The Medicine Wheel and Wilber's spectrum of consciousness – A case study', *The Canadian Journal of Native Studies 33*(1), 2013, 197–16.
6. See Valerie, Earth Ethos, 'Relationships & identity', https://earthethos.net/2018/07/31/relationships-identity/ for graphic depictions of this cycle.
7. Peter A. Levine, *Waking the Tiger: Healing trauma*, North Atlantic Books, Berkeley, California, 2011.
8. Colorado and Cooley, 'Remembering Who We Are'.

WEEK 29

1. Yunkaporta, *Sand Talk*, p. 25.
2. Jo-Anne L. Chrona, First Peoples Principles of Learning, 'Learning involves patience and time', https://firstpeoplesprinciplesoflearning.wordpress.com/learning-involves-patience-and-time/.
3. Lisa Hall, 'Anma, Marpla and Ngapartji Ngapartji: Insights Into how to do Research Together in "Good Faith"', *Learning Communities: International Journal of Learning in Social Contexts*, *22*, 70–80, 2017, p. 76.
4. Allison Reeves, 'Biskanewin Ishkode (The fire that is beginning to stand): Exploring Indigenous mental health and healing concepts and practices for addressing sexual trauma', doctoral dissertation, 2013, p. 55.
5. Nerburn and Gardner (eds), *The Soul of an Indian*.
6. See for example Dr Sarah Holcombe, 'Constraints on researchers acting as change agents', chapter 3 in Janet Hunt, Diane Smith, Stephanie Garling and Will Sanders (eds), *Contested Governance: Culture, power and institutions in Indigenous Australia*, ANU Press, Canberra, 2008.
7. Wikipedia, 'Uluru', https://en.wikipedia.org/wiki/Uluru.
8. Colorado and Cooley, 'Remembering Who We Are', Appendix B.

WEEK 30

1. See for example Wikipedia, 'Gregorian calendar', https://en.wikipedia.org/wiki/Gregorian_calendar.
2. See for example CSIRO, 'About the Indigenous seasonal calendars', https://www.csiro.au/en/research/indigenous-science/Indigenous-knowledge/Calendars/About and University of Melbourne, 'Indigenous astronomy and seasonal calendars', https://indigenousknowledge.unimelb.edu.au/curriculum/resources/indigenous-astronomy-and-seasonal-calendars.
3. See for example Indigenous Weather Knowledge, 'D'harawal calendar', http://www.bom.gov.au/iwk/calendars/dharawal.shtml.
4. For examples of such calendars see Earth Ethos, https://earthethosnet.files.wordpress.com/2019/01/1024px-heathen_holidays.png?w=351&h=248 and Earth Ethos, https://earthethosnet.files.wordpress.com/2019/01/wheelofyear.png?w=284&h=217.
5. The unadapted template can be found at Valerie, Earth Ethos, 'Calendars, Seasons & Cycles', https://earthethos.net/2019/01/31/seasons-cycles/.

WEEK 31

1. Judy Atkinson, *Trauma Trails, Recreating Song Lines: The Transgenerational Effects of Trauma in Indigenous Australia*, Spinifex Press, Melbourne, 2003.
2. Rael, *being & vibration*, p. 15.
3. OED, 'empathy, n', https://www.oed.com/search/dictionary/?scope=Entries&q=empathy.
4. See for example Justin Neuman, The Immanent Frame, 'Ubuntu, reconciliation, and the buffered self', https://tif.ssrc.org/2010/06/07/ubuntu-reconciliation/.
5. Claire E. Oppenheim, 'Nelson Mandela and the Power of Ubuntu', *Religions*, 3(2), 2012, 369–88.
6. Miriam-Rose Ungunmerr-Baumann, 'Dadirri: Inner Deep Listening and Quiet Still Awareness', 2002, http://dadirri.org.au/wp-content/uploads/2015/03/Dadirri-Inner-Deep-Listening-M-R-Ungunmerr-Bauman-Refl1.pdf.

WEEK 32

1. Clarissa Pinkola Estés, *Women Who Run with the Wolves: Myths and Stories of the Wild Woman Archetype*, Ballantine Books, New York, 1996.
2. Wikipedia, 'Hero's journey', https://en.wikipedia.org/wiki/Hero%27s_journey.
3. Wikipedia, 'Martyr', https://en.wikipedia.org/wiki/Martyr and Wikipedia, 'Christian mythology', https://en.wikipedia.org/wiki/Christian_mythology.
4. Wikipedia, 'Damsel in distress', https://en.wikipedia.org/wiki/Damsel_in_distress.
5. Wikipedia, 'American Dream', https://en.wikipedia.org/wiki/American_Dream.
6. Wikipedia, 'Individualism', https://en.wikipedia.org/wiki/Individualism.
7. Wikipedia, 'Might makes right', https://en.wikipedia.org/wiki/Might_makes_right.

WEEK 33

1. David M. Engel, 'Origin Myths: Narratives of Authority, resistance, Disability, and law', *Law and Society Review* 27(4), 785–826, 1993, p. 785.
2. Leeming, *Creation myths of the world*.
3. Marcelo Gleiser, *The Dancing Universe: From Creation Myths to the Big Bang (Understanding Science and Technology)*, Dartmouth Press, Newhaven, 2012.
4. Fred R. Gustafson, *Dancing Between Two Worlds: Jung and the Native American soul*, Mahwah, NJ: Paulist Press International, New Jersey, 1997.
5. Barbara Rogoff, *The Cultural Nature of Human Development*, Oxford University Press, New York, 2003.
6. John P. Wilson and Rhiannon Brywnn Thomas, *Empathy in the Treatment of Trauma and PTSD*, Brunner/Routledge, New York, 2004, p. 1.
7. Peter Fischer, Anne Sauer, Claudia Vogrincic and Silke Weisweiler, 'The ancestor effect: Thinking about our genetic origin enhances intellectual performance', *European Journal of Social Psychology*, 41(1), 11–16, 2011.

WEEK 34

1. Peter Wohlleben, *The Inner Life of Animals: Love, Grief, and Compassion – Surprising Observations of a Hidden World*, Greystone Books, Vancouver, 2016.
2. Dr Lynne Kelly, *The Memory Code: Unlocking the Secrets of the Lives of the Ancients and the Power of the Human Mind*, Atlantic Books, London, 2017, chapter 2.
3. See for example Christina Johnson, Center Spirited, 'Spirit vs Totem vs Power Animal – What is the Difference?', https://centerspirited.com/animal-symbolism/spirit-vs-totem-vs-power-animal/.
4. See for example Minmia, *Under the Quandong Tree*.
5. See for example the film by director Nicole Ma, *Putuparri and the Rainmakers*, Ronin Films, 2015, https://putuparri.com/.

6. See for example Australians Together, 'First Nations kinship', https://australianstogether.org.au/discover/indigenous-culture/kinship.
7. Kelly, *The Memory Code*.
8. See for example Wikipedia, 'Swan maiden', https://en.wikipedia.org/wiki/Swan_maiden.
9. See the 2016 interview with Iraqi-German artist Rashid Salim at Ruya Foundation, 'Reviving Iraq's ancient crafts: interview with the artist Rashad Salim', https://ruyafoundation.org/en/2016/09/3805/?fbclid=IwAR2gDXoM51FzZdH76jDUa6U6y5QVUhbUMKkPtTbqseJOT_Xif5GvOSoojn0.
10. See the 2019 article about Michael Rakowitz at The Brown Daily Herald, 'Conceptual artist discusses Iraqi date palm–inspired cookbook', https://www.browndailyherald.com/article/2019/11/conceptual-artist-discusses-iraqi-date-palm-inspired-cookbook.

WEEK 35
1. Navajo Traditional Teachings, YouTube, 'Walk in Beauty', https://youtu.be/ruYNl-emEic.

WEEK 36
1. Colorado, *Woman Between the Worlds*, p. 128.
2. Nana Veary, *Change We Must: My Spiritual Journey*, The Institute for Zen Studies, Japan, 1989.
3. Joe Vitale and Ihaleakala Hew Len, *Zero Limits: The Secret Hawaiian System for Wealth, Health, Peace, and More*, John Wiley & Sons, New Jersey, 2007.

WEEK 37
1. Polly O. Walker, 'Decolonizing Conflict Resolution: Addressing the Ontological Violence of Westernization', *American Indian Quarterly*, 527–49, 2004.
2. Ross, *Returning to the Teachings*, p. 171 citing an unpublished Hollow Water Position Paper on incarceration.
3. William E. Prendergast, *Treating Sex Offenders: A Guide to Clinical Practice with Adults, Clerics, Children, and Adolescents*, Haworth Press, New York, 1991.
4. For a full documentary about their work see National Film Board of Canada, *Hollow Water*, https://www.nfb.ca/film/hollow_water/ and for a clip from the documentary see Barbara Biggs, YouTube, 'Hollow water', https://youtu.be/MMKIvv5p164.
5. Sawatsky, *The Ethic of Traditional Communities and the Spirit of Healing Justice*, p. 116 quoting a community member.
6. Christine Sivell-Ferri, *The Four Circles of Hollow Water*, Aboriginal Peoples Collection, 1997, https://www.publicsafety.gc.ca/cnt/rsrcs/pblctns/fr-crcls-hllw-wtr/index-en.aspx.
7. Sawatsky, *The Ethic of Traditional Communities and the Spirit of Healing Justice*, p. 116.
8. Robert Yazzie, 'Life Comes from It: Navajo Justice Concepts', *New Mexico Law Revue*, 24, 175–90, 1994, p. 182.
9. Harold Napoleon, *Yuuyaraq: The Way of the Human Being*, Publications Centre, Centre for Cross-Cultural Studies, College of Rural Alaska, University of Alaska Fairbanks, 1991, pp. 27–9.
10. Mary Mueller Shutan, 'Advice: Animism and some unfortunate Wasp houseguests', http://maryshutan.com/advice-animism-and-some-unfortunate-wasp-houseguests/.

WEEK 38
1. National Public Radio, 'How Inuit Parents Teach Kids To Control Their Anger', https://www.npr.org/sections/goatsandsoda/2019/03/13/685533353/a-playful-way-to-teach-kids-to-control-their-anger.

WEEK 39
1. David R. Kopacz, Being Fully Human, 'Lost in the Wilderness of the Body', https://beingfullyhuman.com/.
2. Ibid.

WEEK 40
1. See for example Samrat Dutta, Medium, 'The Story of Narcissus and Echo – Greek Mythology #2', https://medium.com/greek-mythology/the-story-of-narcissus-and-echo-greek-mythology-2-9efa90762a1b and Hope Gillette, Psych Central, 'Narcissus and Echo: The Myth and Tragedy of Relationships with Narcissists', https://psychcentral.com/lib/narcissus-and-echo-the-myth-and-tragedy-of-relationships-with-narcissists#2.
2. Julia Cameron, *The Artist's Way: A Spiritual Path to Higher Creativity*, Pan Books, London, 1993.
3. Estés, *Women Who Run with the Wolves*.
4. Louise Hay, *You Can Heal Your Life*, Hay House Publishing, Sydney, 1984.
5. Yunkaporta, *Sand Talk*, pp. 24–42.
6. Ibid.
7. Ibid.

WEEK 41

1. Ingrid Washinawatok, 'Sovereignty is more than just power', *Indigenous Woman, 2*(6), 23–4, 1999.
2. Sharon H. Venne, 'What is the Meaning of Sovereignty', *Indigenous Woman 2*(6), 27–30, 1999.
3. Hirini Moko Mead, *Tikanga Māori: Living by Māori Values*, rev. ed., Huia Publishers, Wellington, 2016.
4. See for example Hunt, Smith, Garling and Sanders (eds), *Contested Governance*, p. 351; La Donna Harris and Jacqueline Wasilewski, 'Indigeneity, an Alternative Worldview: Four R's (Relationship, Responsibility, Reciprocity, Redistribution) vs. Two P's (Power and Profit). Sharing the Journey Towards Conscious Evolution, *Systems Research and Behavioral Science: The Official Journal of the International Federation for Systems Research, 21*(5), 489–503, 2004; and Irmelin Gram-Hanssen, 'Individual and collective leadership for deliberate transformations: Insights from Indigenous leadership', *Leadership, 17*(5), 519–41, 2021.
5. Taiaiake Alfred, *Peace, Power, Righteousness: An Indigenous Manifesto*, Oxford University Press, Canada, 2008.
6. Talkpoint, 'Sacred Leadership', http://www.talkpoint.com.au/sacredleadership/ and Tjanara Goreng Goreng, 'Tjukurpa Pulka: The Road to Eldership How Aboriginal Culture Creates Sacred and Visionary Leaders', 2018 dissertation thesis available at https://openresearch-repository.anu.edu.au/handle/1885/149431.
7. Robert Kegan, 'Levels of Thinking, Adapted Model', Zaffyre International, Sydney, 2010.
8. Gram-Hanssen, 'Individual and collective leadership for deliberate transformations'.

WEEK 42

1. The Guardian, YouTube, 'Charles Eisenstein: "In a gift economy the more you give, the richer you are"', https://youtu.be/6S1egXWYwXo and Charles Eisenstein, *Sacred Economics: Money, Gift, and Society in the Age of Transition*, North Atlantic Books, Berkeley, California, 2011.
2. Wikipedia, 'Potlatch', https://en.wikipedia.org/wiki/Potlatch.
3. Living Tradition, 'Potlatch', https://umistapotlatch.ca/potlatch-eng.php.
4. Living Tradition, 'English translation of potlatch means "to give"', https://umistapotlatch.ca/potlatch-eng.php.
5. Wikipedia, 'Moka exchange', https://en.wikipedia.org/wiki/Moka_exchange.
6. See for example the movie directed by Charles Naim, *Ongka's Big Moka*; preview available at YouTube, 'Ongka's Big Moka – PREVIEW', https://youtu.be/p7ZlY719p9g.
7. Vipassana Meditation, http://www.dhamma.org/.
8. Brahma Kumaris, http://www.brahmakumaris.org/.

WEEK 43

1. Nap Ministry, 'Rest is Resistance', https://thenapministry.com/.
2. National Public Radio, 'Atlanta-Based Organization Advocates For Rest As A Form Of Social Justice', https://www.npr.org/2020/06/04/869952476/atlanta-based-organization-advocates-for-rest-as-a-form-of-social-justice.
3. The Atlantic, 'Listen: You Are Worthy of Sleep', https://www.theatlantic.com/health/archive/2020/04/you-are-worthy-of-sleep/610996/.
4. Vimeo, *Kanyini*, http://www.kanyini.com/what-is-kanyini.html.
5. Resurgence & Ecologist, 'Kanyini: The four dimensions of aboriginal life', www.resurgence.org/magazine/article132-kanyini.html.
6. Earth Ethos, YouTube, 'Body Relaxation', https://www.youtube.com/watch?v=WBaP1YClNNA.
7. Mindful, 'All Our Relations: Four Indigenous Lessons on Mindfulness', https://www.mindful.org/all-our-relations-four-indigenous-lessons-on-mindfulness/.

WEEK 44

1. Indigenous Values, 'Thanksgiving Address Ganonhanyonh (Words that Come Before All Else): Haudenosaunee Greetings to the Natural World', https://indigenousvalues.org/haudenosaunee-values/thanksgiving-address-ganonhanyonh/.
2. Wikipedia, 'Great Law of Peace', https://en.wikipedia.org/wiki/Great_Law_of_Peace.
3. See for example Campus Ontario, '27. Wampum Belts', https://ecampusontario.pressbooks.pub/indigstudies/chapter/wampum-belts/ and Onondaga Nation, 'Wampum', https://www.onondaganation.org/culture/wampum/.
4. The Soul of the Earth, 'The Haudenosaunee Thanksgiving Address', www.thesouloftheearth.com/the-haudenosaunee-thanksgiving-address/.
5. Dan Abrahamsson, YouTube, 'Haudenosaunee Thanksgiving Address', https://www.youtube.com/watch?v=sWKac3o7isk.
6. Resurgence & Ecologist, 'Kanyini'.
7. See for example Ecology and Society, https://www.ecologyandsociety.org/vol18/iss3/art19/figure2.jpg and 'The 5 Main Elements of Warlpiri Culture', https://tse2.mm.bing.net/th?id=OIP.5-JGWY4IHzouYzo4SWRS-wHaEZ&pid=Api.

8. Wanta (Steve Jampijinpa Patrick), '"Pulya-ranyi": Winds of change', *Cultural Studies Review*, *21*(1), 121–31, 2015.

9. Ibid, p. 128.

10. Kimmerer, *Braiding Sweetgrass*, pp. 28–30.

11. Resurgence & Ecologist, 'Kanyini'.

WEEK 45

1. Christina Pratt, Why Shamanism Now?, 'Healing the Ancestral Lines', https://whyshamanismnow.com/2012/05/healing-the-ancestral-lines/.

2. Malidoma, 'The Legacy of Elder Malidoma Patrice Somé', http://malidoma.com/main/.

3. National Park Service, 'History & Culture', https://www.nps.gov/grsa/learn/historyculture/index.htm.

4. Kimmerer, *Braiding Sweetgrass*, pp. 36–69.

5. Margaret Kovach, *Indigenous Methodologies: Characteristics, Conversations, and Contexts*, University of Toronto Press, Toronto, Canada, 2021, p. 179.

6. Tyson Yunkaporta and Doris Shillingsworth, 'Relationally Responsive Standpoint', *Journal of Indigenous Research*, *8*(2020), 4, 2020.

WEEK 46

1. Nina Martyris, The Salt, '"Paradise Lost": How The Apple Became The Forbidden Fruit', https://www.npr.org/sections/thesalt/2017/04/30/526069512/paradise-lost-how-the-apple-became-the-forbidden-fruit.

2. See for example Shmuel Silinsky, Aish, 'Sin is Not What It Seems', 2009, https://aish.com/48964596.

3. Glenys D. Livingstone, Magoism, 'Crack in the Alienated Colonised Mind', 2020, https://www.magoism.net/2020/03/essay-1-crack-in-the-alienated-colonised-mind-by-glenys-livingstone-ph-d/?fbclid=IwAR0frH17PyDf7wIivBUdMwtP8t77GeeVkndlUpue5lzhkcORLi6WEX0tP1E.

WEEK 47

1. Solomon Monyenye, 'Rites of Passage, Old and New: The role of Indigenous initiation ceremonies and the modern education system, with special reference to Abagusii community of south-western Kenya' in *Thought and Practice in African Philosophy: Selected Papers from the Sixth Annual Conference of the International Society for African Philosophy and Studies*, vol. 5, 2002, p. 191 and Konrad-Adenauer Foundation citing Mircea Eliade, 'Rites and Symbols of Initiation: The Mysteries of Birth and Rebirth', trans. W.R. Trask, Harper and Row, New York, 1965, p. x.

2. Reed A. Morrison, 'Trauma and Transformative Passage', *International Journal of Transpersonal Studies*, *31*(1), 2012, p. 40.

3. Monyenye, 'Rites of Passage, Old and New' citing Eliade, 'Rites and symbols of initiation'.

4. See for example Patrisia Gonzales, *Red medicine: Traditional Indigenous Rites of Birthing and Healing*, University of Arizona Press, Arizona, 2012.

5. See for example L. Dellenborg, 'From pain to virtue, clitoridectomy and other ordeals in the creation of a female person', *Sida Studies*, *24*, 93–101, 2009.

6. Freyia Norling, YouTube, 'Nordic Story Time: A South Sami Saami Creation Story', https://www.youtube.com/watch?v=UTDKeZB7rnM&list=WL&index=16&t=474s.

7. See for example Bradley University Anthropology, 'Satere Mawe Ceremony', https://sites.google.com/fsmail.bradley.edu/buanthro/satere-mawe-ceremony.

8. Wolfgang Kapfhammer, 'Tending the Emperor's Garden: Modes of Human-Nature Relations in the Cosmology of the Sateré-Mawé Indians of the Lower Amazon', *RCC Perspectives*, (5), 75–82, 2012.

WEEK 48

1. Encyclopedia.com, 'Magic: Magic in Indigenous Societies', https://www.encyclopedia.com/environment/encyclopedias-almanacs-transcripts-and-maps/magic-magic-indigenous-societies.

2. See for example Wikipedia, 'Cargo cult', https://en.wikipedia.org/wiki/Cargo_cult and Douglas J. Falen, 'Alter(native) Magic: Race and the Other in Beninese Witchcraft', *Anthropological Forum*, vol. 30, no. 4, pp. 360–76.

3. Brandy Williams, 'White Light, Black Magic: Racism in Esoteric Thought', 2018, http://brandywilliamsauthor.com/wp-content/uploads/2019/07/White-Light-Black-Magic_-Racism-in-Esoteric-Thought.pdf.

4. See for example Kathryn Hilgenkamp and Colleen Pescaia, 'Traditional Hawaiian Healing and Western Influence', *Californian Journal of Health Promotion*, *1*(SI), 34–9, 2003.

WEEK 49

1. For a discussion of the settler role see Earth Ethos, YouTube, 'Settler trauma dialogue', https://www.youtube.com/watch?v=wj5-MTr78V0&t=3s.

2. For a discussion of embodying Indigenous allyship see Earth Ethos, YouTube, 'Weaving Knowledges', https://www.youtube.com/watch?v=N9N7UE7UMqY.

3. Cindy Blackstock, 'The breath of life versus the embodiment of life: indigenous knowledge and western research', *World Indigenous Nations Higher Education Consortium Journal*, 4(1), 67–79, 2007, p. 68.

4. Lynne Kelly, *Knowledge and Power in Prehistoric Societies: Orality, Memory, and the Transmission of Culture*, Cambridge University Press, Cambridge, 2015, p. xvii.

5. See for example Sveiby and Skuthorpe, *Treading Lightly*.

6. See for example Nancy Krieger, 'Embodiment: a conceptual glossary for epidemiology', *Journal of Epidemiology & Community Health*, 59(5), 350–55, 2005, https://jech.bmj.com/content/jech/59/5/350.full.pdf

7. Earth Ethos, YouTube, 'Navigating whiteness dialogue', https://www.youtube.com/watch?v=sYYN-f5m3YI.

8. Earth Ethos, YouTube, 'Identity Politics Dialogue', https://www.youtube.com/watch?v=SxIJAARiZLo.

WEEK 50

1. Australian Broadcasting Corporation, 'Indigenous language and perception', https://www.abc.net.au/radionational/programs/allinthemind/indigenous-language-and-perception/11457578.

2. Law Aspect, 'Natural Law vs. Positive Law', https://lawaspect.com/natural-law-vs-positive-law/.

3. See for example Tonino, 'Robin Wall Kimmerer On Scientific And Native American Views Of The Natural World'.

4. Monica Gratani, Stephen G. Sutton, James R.A. Butler, Erin L. Bohensky and Simon Foale, 'Indigenous environmental values as human values', *Cogent Social Sciences*, 2(1), 1185811, 2016, p. 8.

5. Rael, *Ceremonies of the Living Spirit*, p. 29.

6. See for example Ross, *Returning to the Teachings*.

7. Sawatsky, *The Ethic of Traditional Communities and the Spirit of Healing Justice*.

WEEK 52

1. Vine Deloria Jr, *Custer Died for Your Sins: An Indian Manifesto*, University of Oklahoma Press, Oklahoma, 1988, p. 39.

2. CBC, '"The best medicine": 10 Indigenous comedians on how they use humour for healing', https://www.cbc.ca/arts/the-best-medicine-10-indigenous-comedians-on-how-they-use-humour-for-healing-1.6082789.

3. Shannon Leddy, 'In a good way: Reflecting on humour in indigenous education', *Journal of the Canadian Association for Curriculum Studies*, 16(2), 10–20, 2018.

ABOUT THE AUTHOR

1. Nordfriisk Instituut, 'Nordfrieslandlexicon', https://www.nordfriiskfutuur.eu/nordfrieslandlexikon/friesisches-manifest/.

2. Valerie, Earth Ethos, 'Jews' Indigenous Roots, https://wordpress.com/post/earthethos.net/1336.

Acknowledgements

With gratitude for all of the ancestors and lands who supported this book to come into being, all of the knowledge-sharers cited within these pages, and especial thanks to Kimia and Ellis, who read as I wrote, and my husband Lukas, who lives the teachings with me.

About the author

Dr Valerie Cloud Clearer Schwan Ringland is a Frisian[1]–Sumerian/ Jewish[2] woman. Her spiritual name is Wulkenkloorjer (Cloud Clearer) because she works to clear internal clouds polluting the mind and transform sh*t life experiences into fertiliser for learning and healing. She is an Indigenous scientist, medicine woman, mother, partner, researcher, writer, space holder, friend, caretaker and community member.

Valerie has lived experience knowledge of intense trauma, grief and loss, health challenges, spiritual crises and conflict resolution. She has more than a decade of experience in healing work and has done apprenticeships in Indigenous healing methods, including ceremonial dancing, earthing ceremonies, dreamwork, sweat lodge ceremonies and sacred circle keeping.

In terms of Western education she has a PhD in social work, for which she did a dissertation on Indigenous trauma healing, a JD in law, BA in maths and certifications in mediation and restorative justice. She also has more than a decade of experience in facilitation, research and social policy and practice work around the world, including in Australia, the US, India, South Africa and Peru.

Valerie founded Earth Ethos in 2018, which has allowed her to create and teach courses such as 'Indigenous science research methods' at UPeace, do bespoke research projects such as on childbirth as a woman's traditional spiritual initiation, blog and write articles, offer healing and support work with individuals, families and groups and facilitate community gatherings.

Index

climate change 78, 83, 250
cognitive dissonance 113, 263
colonialism 50–1, 57
colonisation 1, 265; impacts
of 120
communities 47–8; values-
based 131
compassion 17; narcissism and
217; Western systems and
161; wounds and limitations
and 111
compromise 201
conflict resolution 199–202;
circle ceremonies and 201;
exercise on 202; exercise on
conflict with lore 268
connection 4; between
ceremony and the Earth
32; creation and 50; Earth
and 27, 45; exercise for 32;
Indigenous roots and 51;
land and 46; other people
and 45, 243; with self 60; see
also interconnectedness
consciousness 61–8; altered 62,
63, 65–8, 120–2; altering of
148; cleansing to alter 67–8;
collective 232; exercise 66;
raising of 132; tools to alter
65–6
control 75, 83, 103, 128
core values 13–20; anger and
206; awareness of 260;
boundaries and 117; creation
stories and 180; discernment
and 190; embodiment of 15,
36; exercise for 15; gaining
of 18; illumination of 54;
impact of 14; myths and 177
cortisone, cycles 23; function
of 23
cosmology 53–8, 145, 253;
ceremony and 65; creation
stories and 72; dualism in
55; exercise on 55, 56, 188;
Indigenous 73, 86, 271;
trauma and 60, 62; Western
57, 265; worldview and 4, 54
creation 237; exercise for 55,
250; separation from 103,
106; healing emerging from
67, 266; understanding of
265
creation stories 54, 57–8,
180–1, 252; common 57–8,
180; exercise 58, 105, 181;
foundation of cosmology

and 70–2; illuminating core
values 54; political identities
and 58; trickster and 131; see
also big bang theory, Judeo-
Christian
cross-quarter days 2, 166, 282;
exercise with 167
cultural appropriation 150, 256
cultures 179–83, 257;
alienation 97; appropriation
of 150; beliefs of 4;
colonialisation of 182;
commonalities of 1; creation
stories and 180; exercise
36, 58, 124, 181, 213, 258;
exercise on creating a
cultural connection 183;
exercise on cultural and
ancestral healing through
grief 213; gift culture 224
and see gift economy; grief in
212–13; identity within 182;
initiation ceremonies in 252;
integrity of 261; shadow of
78; totemic systems in 186;
trauma in 182
cycles 164; addiction 120;
Earth's 91, 103, 210, 252;
exercise on 137, 165, 167; of
violence 154; sleep 23, 103

dadirri 170, 230
darkness 70–2, 149, 180;
constellations of 50, 218;
cosmology and 72, 256;
exercise 71; into light 57, 70,
180; Unknown 67
death 96–101; ceremonies for
99; Earth's cycle and 154;
exercise on 99; meditation
exercise for 100; spiritual 98,
110, 210; today is a good day
to die exercise 101; trauma
and 97–8
decay 96–101; exercise on 99;
process of 9
decolonisation 123, 166, 230,
248, 256, 265
deficit-based thinking 126, 128
denial 60, 83, 86, 117, 131,
149, 154
desires 39, 83, 100, 125–9, 150;
exercise on 29, 211
discernment 82, 117, 189–93;
exercise on 191, 233;
strengthening of 190, 192–3,
227, 243, 263

disconnection 86, 93, 217, 242;
exercise on 46; from Earth
23, 61, 86
dis-ease 50–1, 60, 206–7
dissociation 61, 65; exercise on
63, 66
divination 256; exercise to
divine your medicine wheel
137
dreams 34, 75, 170, 209, 257,
266; exercise with 144
drumming 65, 230, 257;
exercise with 63, 93
dualism 55, 70, 82, 83, 197;
see also black and white
thinking

Earth, cycles of 91, 103, 210,
252; source for law 265–6;
see also Mother Earth
earthing see grounding
Echo wounds 215–17, 218;
exercise on 216; see also
narcissism
egalitarianism 220
ego 34, 50–1, 60, 83; exercise
with 52
Elders 220–22; conflict with
201; exercise on 222;
leadership of 221; spending
time with 51
elements 10, 13, 135–40;
exercise 140; honouring of
138–9
embodiment 259–63; exercise
for 20; exercise for place
embodiment 263; exercise
on embodied memory
aids 262; exercise on
embodiment of holiness
250; reflection on 261, 263
emotions, anger 203–7;
empathy see empathy;
exercise on cultural and
ancestral healing through
grief 213; exercise on grief
and regret 207; grief 208–13;
handling of 98; logic of
117; regret 210; release of
negative 107; resentment
207; triggering of 97–8
empathy 17, 108–13; definition
of 109, 170; exercise on
66, 109, 113; lack of 110;
rejection and 215; unpacking
the gift of 110–13
energy 2, 11, 22, 42;

channelling of *see*
channelling; connection
of with Earth and Sky
11; exercise on healing
power dynamics through
channelling energy 156; is it
mine? exercise 191; primal
87; trauma and 61
environments 6; empaths and
112–13; environmentalist
47; exercise on 12, 105, 155,
172, 188, 193; impact of 18,
45, 88, 103, 112, 116
equinoxes 2, 8, 164, 166, 281;
exercise on 167
evolution 34, 55, 57

faith 72, 75, 80–4, 98; blind 81;
definition of 81; flow and
81; integrity and 115, 117;
maintaining of 83, 106, 126,
153; Unknown and 110
Father Sky 10; iconography of
55; medicine wheel and 10;
physical world of 106
fear 60–1, 190–1; culture
and 207; exercise on 191;
existential 81; survival 88,
116; trauma and 61, 98, 131,
190, 217; Unknown and
75, 97
flexibility 220
flow 74–9; blocks in 42, 76,
161; drumming to assist 65;
exercise on 68, 77; faith and
81; randomness as 75; state
of 16, 39, 65, 103, 159, 209,
234, 244; Unknown and 75
footprints 22
forgiveness 133, 194–8, 200;
collective 196; exercise on
198; justice and 195–6
four directions 10–11, 142;
exercise with 11, 12, 144, 146

generosity 45, 177, 219–22,
226–28, 239; exercise on
222, 228; reciprocity and 45;
sovereignty and 220; *see also*
gift economy
gift economy 223–8; definition
of 224; exercise on 225, 228
god/s 8, 30, 72, 166, 249, 252;
exercise 55; let go and let 39
governance 220–1, 224, 227; *see
also* sovereignty
gratitude 236–40, 242; exercise

on 22, 32, 238, 240; gift
economy and 224, 227;
natural world and 129, 239
greed 50, 128; trickster and
131; *see also* Wetiko
Greetings to the Natural
World 237
grief 208–13, 242; abuse
and 87, 126, 207, 212;
boundaries and 115, 117,
133; causes of 210; cultural
212; exercise on grief and
regret 207; intergenerational
212
grounding 1, 21–5, 86, 248;
authenticity and 18, 86, 260;
belonging and 243; exercise
on 24, 25, 66; methods to
effect 22, 24–5; reducing
anxiety through 23
guru worship 149

healing, ancestral 35, 123–4;
energy 257; exercise on
cultural and ancestral
healing through grief 213;
flow and 75; impulse for
112; physical 257; psychic
256; sound 257; story 257;
symbolic 257; through
ceremony 65; through
knowledge 67
health: ecosystem and 266;
human 266; physical 28;
spiritual 28
heart 10, 97; as centre of
medicine wheel 11, 60, 136,
153; centredness in 10, 16,
18, 86
hierarchy 8, 126; exercise 52
holiness 246–50; definition of
247; desecration and 248;
Earth's resources and 248;
integration of 249; reflection
on 247, 250
hollow bones 11; *see also*
channelling
Honourable Harvest
128–9; exercise 129; *see also*
reciprocity
Ho'oponopono 197; exercise
197
hope 83; faith and 81
human nature 47, 54,
86–7, 103, 249, 265; exercise
honouring 32; exercise on
52; sin and 248; trickster

and 131
humility 17, 195, 221; human
nature and 265; I don't know
mind and 72; leadership and
221; spiritual traps and 149;
trickster and 132, 275
humour 6, 274–8; exercise
on 277, 278; trickster and
132–3; use of 275–6

I don't know mind 72, 75
identity 57, 112; beliefs and
132, 239; central myths
and 177; empathy and 110,
170; exercise on ancestral
identity and 124; exercise on
central myth 178; exercise
on embodiment and identity
263; exercise on empathy
113; exercise on initiation
and identity 254; exercise
on integrating Western
and Indigenous science
273; exercise on integrity
and 118, 270; exercise on
non-humans and totemic
connection 188; exercise
on projecting identity onto
another 197; in wounds
153–4; initiation and 254;
land and 57, 92; self-worth
and 116–17, 215; shame
in 120, 153–4; trauma and
61, 200
imagination 25, 38–43, 106;
empathy and 109–110
inclusivity 158, 221; empathic
listening and 170
indigeneity 1, 34–5, 57, 92;
exercise on 188
Indigenous cosmologies
2; creation 5; cultures
see cultures; governance
221, 224, 227; grounding
23; justice 195–6;
knowledge 239; leadership
221–2; meaning of 4, 57;
mythologies 57; roots 4, 128;
social science 1
Indigenous science: addiction
and 119–24; altar work
and 39–40, 141–6;
ancestor honouring within
33–7; anger and 203–7;
belonging and 47, 241–5;
birth and rebirth in 90–5;
birthright of 6; boundaries

and 114–18; calendars
and 163–8; ceremonies in
26–32, 138; communication
with non-humans and
185; conflict resolution
and 199–202; connections
within 31; core values in
13–19; cosmology in 53–8;
creation as a basis of 55;
creation stories in 70; culture
and 179–83; darkness in
70, 72, 149; death and
96–101; decay and 96–101;
desire and need in 125–9;
discernment in 189–93;
dissociation in 65; elements
and 135–40; embodiment
of 115–16, 259–63;
empathy in 108–13, 170;
faith in 80–4; forgiveness
and 194–8; generosity
and 219–22; gift economy
and 223–8; governance in
220–1, 224, 227; gratitude
and 236–40; greed and
128; grief and 208–13;
grounding in 21–5; healing
in 6; holiness and 246–50;
holism of 6, 57; Honourable
Harvest and 128–9;
honouring of processes of
94; humour in 6, 274–8;
identities 58; imagination
in 38–43; initiation and
251–4; integration of 272,
273; integrity in 269–73;
interconnectedness in 47;
introduction to 3–8; law and
justice in 264–8; listening
and 169–72; magic in 38–43,
255–8; manifestation and
75; meaning of 6; medicine
wheel in 9–12; narcissism
and 214–18; non-humans
and 184–8; patience and
157–62; placenta in 91, 92;
power and 152–6; rebirth
and 90–5; reciprocity and
45–8, 128–9; relationships
and 185–6; rest and stillness
in 229–35; rituals in 26–32,
138; sovereignty in 220;
spiritual traps and 147–51;
stories and 173–8; survival
strategies and 85–9; time in
see synchronicity; totemic
forgiveness and 194–8;

trauma and 59–63; trickster
and 131–4; Wetiko in 49–52
individuality 153, 260; see also
lived experience
information see knowledge
initiation 251–4; exercise on
254; spiritual 252; teaching
myths and values 253
in-mateship 128
instant gratification 158
integrity 269–73; boundaries
and 115–16; cultural 261;
exercise for 118, 270, 273;
gift economy and 227; see
also boundaries
intensity 148
interconnectedness 4; Earth
and 45; Indigenous science
and 47; land and 58;
listening and 171; of being
153; other people and 237;
with place 47; world and 27;
see also connection
intuition 10, 18; exercise using
7, 12, 36, 89, 137, 144, 156

journeys 4, 10, 34, 107, 112,
161, 170, 272; death 95,
98, 257; drum 63, 93, 230;
leadership 221
Judeo-Christian 55, 57, 204;
creation myth 57, 180
judgement 86, 88, 128, 195,
227; anger and 116–17,
206; discernment and 190;
exercise 111; existential 47,
149, 153, 195; punishment
and 200, 265; social 224
justice 195–6, 204–6, 230,
265–7; Indigenous 47,
195–6, 267; restorative 47,
Western 195–6, 265

k'é 200
Kanyini 232, 239
karma 34
kinship 51, 185, 232, 257;
exercise on 181; see also non-
humans
knowledge 4, 6, 67, 92, 115,
161, 193; lived experience
260–1; sharing of 142, 150,
260–1; traditional 185–6,
220, 232, 239, 257, 260;
Unknown and 73

land, connection and

disconnection with 46,
239; exercise for 25, 46,
56; exercise for learning to
survive where you live 193;
exercise on holy land 247;
finding peace on 243–4;
gift economy and 239; holy
56, 247–8, 249; identity
and 57; loss of 212; pain of
45–6; interconnectedness
with 58; reclaiming of 248;
sacredness of 57; sovereignty
and 220; see also place
language 70, 76, 182, 185, 239,
243, 257, 266; exercise on
183, 268
law 185–6, 257, 264–8; exercise
on 268; Indigenous 221,
265–6; positive 265; source
of 265; upholding of 195–7,
266–7; Western view of 265;
see also governance, Ngurra-
kurlu
leadership 60, 220–2, 227;
exercise on 222, 228
light see darkness
light-heartedness 6, 277; see
also humour
limitations 17–18, 54, 72, 76,
256, 261; exercise on 17, 268
listening 169–72; deep 176,
230, 232, 239; empathic
170–1, 177; exercise on 172;
receptivity and 170; sacred
circles and 171; sit spots
and 171
lived experience 18, 106, 115,
154, 170, 174, 185, 260–1,
263; exercise with 122;
initiation and 252
logic 161; exercise on mental
logic 162
lore 34, 86, 177, 185–6, 257,
265–6; exercise on 268
loss 212; see also grief
lower world 106

magic 38–43, 255–8;
components of 256–7;
definition of 256; exercise on
skills and tools of 258
materialism 65, 153, 250;
spiritual 65, 68
mateship 128
medicine person 60, 186, 256
medicine wheel 9–12; addiction
in 120; altar work and 142,

self-worth 50, 83–4, 110–11,
116–17, 128, 154, 206,
242–3; exercise on magical
tools and skills to honour
self 258; narcissism and 217;
rest and 230
separation 50, 103–4, 210;
exercise on 105; initiation
and 252–3
shadow 74–9, 82, 153, 243;
cultural 78; definition of
75–6; understanding of
76, 78
shaman *see* medicine person
shaman's illness 61, 97
shame 83, 110–11, 120,
128; ancestral 123, 126;
boundaries and 116–17;
exercise with 52, 277;
healing 226, 249, 276;
offending and 153–4
shrines 39
silence 148, 158, 170, 234;
exercise on 235
sin 154, 248–9
sit spots 171; exercise 172
sleep *see* rest
solstices 2, 8, 138, 166, 281;
exercise with 167
soul loss 61
soul retrieval 217, 257
sovereignty 1, 220, 265; *see also*
governance
spirit world 60
spiritual initiation *see* initiation
spiritual traps 147–51;
ambition 149–50; black and
white thinking 131, 149,
192; cultural appropriation
150; exercise on 151; guru
worship 149; spiritual
businesses 150; spiritual
bypass 148
stillness 170–1, 229–35;
exercise on 172, 178, 231,
233; silence and 234; *see
also* rest
stories 173–8; belonging and
243; creation *see* creation
stories; exercise on 175,
176; exercise on central
myth 178, 181; exercise on
projecting identity onto
another 197; owning the
storyteller 174; teachings of
265; *see also* myths
strength 7, 35; in self exercise

on 20, 24
supernatural world 6, 55, 57,
252, 256
supremacy 220; exercise about
52; human 51–2, 54; white
174, 263
survival needs 19, 88; exercise
127; exercise to learn to
survive where you live 193
survival strategies 85–9, 120;
exercise on 89
synchronicity 102–7; exercise
for 105; human nature
and 103; non-human
interconnection exercise 107;
patience and 159; seasons
and cycles and 103–4; time
measurement and 16,103;
way of being and 106

Thanksgiving Address *see*
Greetings to the Natural
World
time 6, 10, 16, 165
tools, exercise on 258; magical
257
totem 142, 185–7, 257; exercise
with 124, 144, 188; pole 185
trauma 59–63; abuse and 45–6;
addiction and 120; ancestral
34, 35; ancestral trauma
exercise 191; colonisation
and 51; definition of 60;
exercise 63; healing of
60–2; initiation and 252;
intergenerational 60, 120,
174
trees 40–1, 51, 142, 239;
exercise to make a tree altar
41; tree of life 18, 91
trickster 131–4; dark side of
131; discernment and 82,
193, 195, 263; exercise on
134; mind and 104, 153,
161, 163
trust 18, 82; definition of 82;
exercise with 77; faith and
82; in life 60, 75, 83; of
others 18, 71–2, 78, 149; of
self 16, 60, 217; *see also* faith
truth 81–3, 98, 111, 271;
Truth and Reconciliation
Commission 170

ubuntu 170
Unknown 11, 69–73; death and
97; exercise on 71, 73, 77;

leap of faith into 81–3, 110
unsafety *see* safety
upper world 106

values *see* core values
victimhood 50, 52, 72, 82, 88,
98, 106, 153, 154
violence 87, 128, 153–4, 253;
cycle of 154; in the body
35, 192
visualisation 10, 25, 133, 207,
256–7; exercise with 7, 25,
156
vitality 6, 136, 243; exercise
with 24, 26
Vitruvian man 10, 18
vulnerability 16, 97, 115, 121,
171; *see also* safety

wealth 224–7; exercise on 225
Western science 6, 34, 40,
55; dissociation and 65–7;
energy and 86; exercise on
integration with Indigenous
science 273; knowledge
and 260; law and 265–6;
placenta and 92; sovereignty
and 220; trauma and 60; *see
also* big bang theory
Wetiko 49–52, 58, 196, 243;
addiction and 121; collective
126, 196, 212; definition
of 50; exercise about 52;
healing of 51; power and
153
wheel of the year 10, 166
whiteness 55, 57, 70, 174, 263;
ancestral exercise 58
worldview *see* cosmology
worth *see* self-worth